"This is a remarkable book, not only written skillfully but with a rare mix of loving attention, humor, practical wisdom, and a deep sense that two people are taking the journey into Alzheimer's together."

— **Reeve Lindbergh**, author of *Under A Wing, No More Words: A Journal of My Mother, Anne Morrow Lindbergh*, and many books for children

"The Majesty of Your Loving is a story of courage, love, and growing wisdom in the face of Alzheimer's. Olivia Hoblitzelle charts the course of her husband's cognitive loss and their deepening insights into life and death, intimacy and separation. I was moved and inspired by this heartful and wonderfully honest account of the daily challenges of opening to the unknown. Olivia shares with us the gift of awareness and the grace of love."

— **Joseph Goldstein**, author of *One Dharma*
Founder / Director of Insight Meditation Society

"This powerful book guides us through the tender last years of a great and wise man who awakened on the journey through the loss of his mental acuity.... A book of great inspiration, courage, and hope, every word rings with truth, kindness, and the beauty of the human spirit."

— **Roshi Joan Halifax**, author
Founder / Director of Upaya Zen Center

D0963462

"This beautiful book is unlike any other personal account of living with Alzheimer's disease that I have ever read. After thirty years of practice in this field, The Majesty of Your Loving changed the way I think about Alzheimer's disease. . .. This heuristic, epiphany provoking, poetically written book offers patients and families practical insights into how they can live their love more fully and derive meaning from amidst the heartbreak of a mind-robbing illness."

— **Paul Raia**, Ph.D., Director of Patient Care and Family Support Alzheimer's Association, Massachusetts Chapter

"The majesty of loving comes through on every page of this wise and touching book. It has helped me to remember life's precious gifts and fleeting yet miraculous nature. I heartily recommend this teaching memoir, rich with memorable life lessons and poignant anecdotes, to anyone wishing to deal with life's most difficult passages in a deeply meaningful and beautifully growthful way."

— **Lama Surya Das**, author of *Buddha Is as Buddha Does* and *Awakening the Buddha Within*, Founder of the Western Buddhist Teachers Network

"A masterful work full of courage, honesty and above all love. Invaluable for all of us humans; especially so if you have a contemplative bent. I completed the book, put it down and was so moved that I could not speak for hours."

— **Larry Rosenberg**, author of *Breath By Breath and Living in the Light of Death*; Founder and Guiding Teacher, Cambridge Insight Meditation Center.

THE MAJESTY
OF YOUR LOVING

A Couple's Journey Through Alzheimer's

OLIVIA AMES HOBLITZELLE

Green Mountain Books GMB Cambridge, Massachusetts

Published by
Green Mountain Books
P.O. Box 381487, Cambridge, MA 02238-1487

FIRST EDITION

Cover and interior design by Yachun Peng

Grateful acknowledgment goes to the following for permission to reprint quotes:

Excerpt from "The Mouse and the Camel" from *The Essential Rumi*, translated by Coleman
Barks. San Francisco: HarperSanFrancisco. © 1995 by Coleman Barks. Reprinted by permission
of the author.

"Vacillation" by W.B. Yeats. Reprinted with the permission of Scribner, an imprint of Simon
& Schuster Adult Publishing Group, from THE COLLECTED WORKS OF W.B. YEATS,
VOLUME I: THE POEMS, Revised edited by Richard J. Finneran. Copyright © 1933 by The
Macmillan Company; copyright renewed 1961 by Bertha Georgie Yeats. All rights reserved.

Excerpt from "Fern Hill" from *The Poems of Dylan Thomas*, published by New Directions
Publishing Corp. Copyright © 1971. Used with permission.

Excerpt from "Dance Me to the End of Love" by Leonard Cohen. Copyright © 1992
Sony/ATV Songs, LLC. All rights administered by Sony/ATV Tree Music Publishing. 8 Music
Square West, Nashville, TN 37203.

"I Can't Help But Wonder (Where I'm Bound)." Words and Music by Tom Paxton. Copyright
© 1963; Renewed 1991 Cherry Lane Music Publishing Company, Inc. (ASCAP) and
Dimensional Music Of 1091 (ASCAP). Worldwide Rights for Dimensional Music Of 1091
Administered by Cherry Lane Music Publishing Company, Inc. International Copyright
Secured. All Rights Reserved.

Library of Congress Cataloging-in-Publication Data
Hoblitzelle, Olivia Ames
The majesty of your loving : a couple's journey through Alzheimer's / by Olivia
Ames Hoblitzelle.
13-digit ISBN: 978-0-9793218-0-1
10-digit ISBN: 0-9793218-0-8
1. Death & Dying 2. Buddhist Psychology
I. Title: The Majesty of Your Loving. II. Title

CONTENTS

FOR HOB
and for Ethan and Laura

Harrison Hoblitzelle known as "Hob" and
Olivia Ames Hoblitzelle in 1999

Photography: Chuck Dean

FOREWORD

Alzheimer's. Who wants to hear this dreaded word and its dreaded implications? Especially in the context of a family member, a friend, or yourself? And yet this disease is now an unfortunate risk of living a long life in our society.

In the case of Harrison Hoblitzelle, it came relatively early, at the age of 72. No one asks for this, ever, at any age. But what can we do when it arises as an actuality in our family or in ourselves? How can we meet the calamity of the threat; the loss of everything we hold dear and that most fundamentally characterizes us or someone we know and love? How can we even contemplate the loss of the memories of the near and sometimes also the distant past, of the ability to be reliably oriented, effortlessly and consistently, within time and space, to say nothing of the web of our relationships and purposes? How can we contemplate the loss of what we take to be our mind and what it knows, the loss of one's very personhood if you will? What, if anything, is the karmic assignment here? How are we called to be in relationship to such a turn of fate when it happens to someone we love?

These are questions that have a horrific urgency to them when Alzheimer's all of a sudden becomes a personal reality. They beg for intelligent suggestions and approaches if not answers, for pointers to possible ways of being real and spacious in the face of what is befalling our loved one, ourselves, and our family. Behind such questions no doubt lies the hope that perhaps there is some kind of sensible and trustworthy coordinate system that we might discover and embrace, one that we can count on and steer by through the inevitable maelstrom of this disease. There is. Olivia Hoblitzelle offers us a robust example of it here, an approach that includes broad permission and encouragement for us to adapt it creatively to our own circumstances. The particulars of her experiences with Hob, as well as her nuanced reflections, suggestions, and seed thoughts at the end of each chapter are inclusive and all-embracing, inviting us to ponder and feel our own ways through these unpredictable waters. These gentle and inspiring encouragements are not based on any rigid adherence to belief systems, but rather in the cultivation of the heart. They skillfully remind us of the key virtue of kindness, and the power of cultivating self-compassionate intimacy with our own mind states and body states, especially in times of great upset and difficulty.

For a care-giver relative, dealing with Alzheimer's disease is virtually a mission impossible, and yet the assignment is raining down on more and more of us every day. I witnessed my father succumb to it and incrementally lose large swatches of his mind over eight years. Yet his heart if anything grew larger and came more to the fore. These were years of surprising closeness and love as well as maddening grief, loss, and frustration.

I have known Olivia Hoblitzelle a long time. We were students of the Korean Zen teacher, Seung Sahn, together, as was Hob, in the mid-seventies. Later, Olivia worked with me for a time as a colleague in the Stress Reduction Clinic at the Medical Center, conducting with great skill and empathy intake interviews with people who had been referred by their physicians for the clinic's training program in mindfulness. Although I have known her a long time, I would not have said I knew Olivia well—that is, until I read this book. Now, just from reading her recounting of life with Hob after they received the diagnosis, and her flashbacks into the past and happier times, I feel I know her very well, in the most important ways. I find myself admiring her enormously for how she held herself and her experience during Hob's decline, and for what she has done here so eloquently to make her compelling perspective available to others in similar situations. I stand in awe of her honesty, determination, courage and, if she doesn't mind my saying so, of the majesty of *her* loving, not just of Hob, but of life, and of hard-won integrity. I also stand in awe of her gentle voice as both writer and teacher.

Now Olivia shares with the world this story of herself and Hob facing Alzheimer's together and, and at the same time, invariably also alone. This book is a record and a map that many of us will find tremendously useful and inspiring. Within these pages, you will see and feel how extraordinary the man she was married to was, how admirable his values and his work, and how keen his sense of humor, even in the face of his own disintegration. And you will see how extraordinary Olivia herself is. Ultimately, I believe that it will help you to realize that you, the reader, by virtue of being human, are no less extraordinary than they are. That is certainly what Olivia would say.

It is all very ordinary, this living and dying, this being human and having to face the unexpected and the unwanted sooner or later. The challenge really is, can we be here for the living and the dying in ways that have integrity, and that are truly loving and nurturing—and that includes ourselves and all our warts and pimples, no matter what fate befalls us, as both Hob and Olivia understood and worked at embodying against huge odds?

What I find most inspiring in this book is Olivia's commitment, and Hob's, each in their own way, to be present with their experiences and to find ways to make meaning out of what at first blush has nothing but horror in it. And to chart these waters carefully and precisely so that others who have to navigate them can indeed have something of a compass and map by which to steer around and through the shoals of fear and frustration, the rocks of anger and impatience, and the currents of sadness, bewilderment, and despair. It seems an impossible task, and yet Olivia not only demonstrates that it is possible, but gives us remarkably useful suggestions for handling the various phases of the disease with grace and good will, as a meditation practice in its own right, perhaps the ultimate way in which to be true to oneself, to life, and to those we love.

— **Jon Kabat-Zinn, August 2007**

ACKNOWLEDGMENTS

As I remember those who accompanied us during Hob's last years, I'm struck yet again by the eternal truth of interconnectedness and all the ways we touch one another's lives. Boundless thanks to each of you—our fellow travelers on this journey.

From my three circles, past and present: Ethan and Elise Hoblitzelle, Louise Cochran, Jimmy Levinson, Susan and Joel Brown-Zimmerman, Prajna Hallstrom, Donna Svrluga, Demaris Wehr, Priscilla Mueller, Richard Griffin, and to Hob's two spiritual brothers, Emerson Stamps and Charles Busch, a deep bow of gratitude and thanks.

Boundless thanks to my teachers: Domo Geshe Rinpoche, Tulku Thondup, Rodney Smith, Jack Kornfield, Christina Feldman, Trudy Goodman, Narayan Liebenson-Grady, Tara Brach, Jon Kabat-Zinn, Sharon Salzberg, Joseph Goldstein, Corrado Pensa, Larry Rosenberg, Thich Nhat Hanh, and a number of others.

Thanks to beloved friends and family: Rae Barclay (Ani Tsering Lhamo), Natalie Rogers, Linda Coe, Sam Fisk, Robert Jonas, Ferris Buck, Ned Kelley, Margot Wilkie, Alice O. Howell,

Anne Nash, Dan Jones, Anne Burling, Arnie Kotler, Therese Fitzgerald, Ray Montgomery, Shannon Gilligan, Cathey Busch, Sam Black, Jack Engler, Ro Gordon, Niya Yannatos, Emilie Welles, Chaitanya Samways, Andrew Weiss, Judith Abbott, Paula Green, Elizabeth Koundakjian, Veronica Jochim von Moltke, Ananda Wall, and especially to Keith Taylor for his support in the home stretch. A crown of laurels to Ildri Ginn for her great generosity in offering me the Blue Door as a writing refuge and her gifts as wise elder.

Oakes and Louise Ames, Ned Ames, Jane Sokolow, Amyas and Lucia Ames, Randy Bak, the cousins, and especially Joanie Ames who gave endless support and light-heartedness at many welcome as well as critical times.

For those who helped as caregivers and helpers: Sean Greene, Jim Perkins, Audrey Moseley, Barbara Elsbeth, Simon Shaize, Ann Cason, Roger Guest, the Windhorse team, Emily and Libby Scoppettulo, Jocylyne Chevry. and above all, Diane Thomas (another crown of laurels) whose incomparable gifts brightened our lives for three years.

And those who held us together, body and soul: Emily Osgood, Sue Putnam, Marilyn Sladek, Peter Faust, Jim McCormick, John di Carlo, John Schlorholtz, Jean Freebody, Christine Aquilino, Lisa Wheeler, Carol Gordon, Margaret Sweet, Mary Jonaitis, Michael Adams, Phuli Cohan, Alex Bingham, Loring Conant, and Bruce Price.

Thanks for editorial, publication, and practical support to Marcia Yudkin, Anne Edelstein, Eden Steinberg, and especially

Ceci Miller and Terry Hiller, my editors on the CeciBooks team. For the beautiful video *Hob's Odyssey*, a deep bow and thanks to Janet Boynton. Also to my assistant, Margaret Harding, who is something between a wizard and a saint. And finally, Barbara McCollough, my writing buddy, who has been with me the whole way with her humor, insights, and inspiration.

Ethan and Laura, our son and daughter, thank you for coming into our lives. Blessings and boundless love to you both.

INTRODUCTION

There's an old saying that what happens to us in life is not as important as how we handle it. At some point, each of us will come to the pivotal crossroads where we either receive a serious diagnosis or know that we are living the last chapter of our lives. Some spiritual traditions suggest that this last chapter—leading up to and including the moment of death—is the most important one of all.

That may strike us as a pretty heavy prospect, but if we shift the lens of understanding just a little, we can entertain the possibility that this most poignant phase of life also has its opportunities, surprises, moments of grace, and hidden blessings. This is one of the premises of *The Majesty of Your Loving*.

My husband, known by his nickname "Hob," was diagnosed with Alzheimer's when he was in his early seventies. With the help of his nature, his life's work, and, above all, his lightheartedness and sense of humor, he negotiated the difficult passages of this illness with insight and inspiring perspectives. Given the tremendous challenges of Alzheimer's, he naturally had his share of difficult times—of frustration, discouragement, and fear. Yet one day, referring to the challenge of it all, he declared emphatically:

"This is the best education I've ever had!"

To be honest, there was an expletive before the word "education." As Hob never swore, this was a dramatic statement. What could he possibly mean? How could a heartbreaking illness be an education, especially one like Alzheimer's—or any other form of dementia—that gradually steals away the mind? In this cryptic statement, loaded with irony and feeling, he was referring to *how* one handles life, especially when confronted with relentless loss and increasing disability.

The compelling question is: How do we accept the process of aging, diminishment, and loss? In the case of dementia, how do we find meaning amidst what appears to be a ruthless and meaningless process? Is it possible to find something redeeming while living with a heartbreaking illness? Hob and I lived tenderly with these questions. *The Majesty of Your Loving* shares some of the ways we found peace with them.

I had to write about this experience. Writing felt like a calling—one so strong there was no way I could have ignored it. Both Hob and I had been trained extensively in psychology and meditation. We had worked and taught in these fields for many years. I knew that the wisdom gained from our experience would shed light on the darkest moments. From the beginning, I sensed that there would be insight, learning, and wisdom that we could share with others.

I began to write, albeit irregularly. I jotted down Hob's observations. I reflected on the careening, unpredictable journey we were on. Periodically I would remind Hob that I was writing and that his voice would be part of a book.

Shortly before his death, I was sitting beside his bed late one evening, as I did every evening. Although he could no longer speak, I had a sure sense that we were deeply in touch, connected at a level beyond words. Sometimes he would stir slightly or squeeze my hand. These felt like return messages. Usually this was a time for silence or maybe quiet singing, but that night, certain that he could hear me, I said, "Hob, I want to make a promise. I'm going to complete this writing. Your voice will be part of it because I've written down things you've said and about how you've handled it. It will become a book—hopefully, something helpful to others."

These words assumed the force of a contract between us. At the same time, I began to feel our connection with everyone who was dealing with mental loss. You, the reader, somehow became a fellow traveler on this most challenging of journeys.

Hob was a gifted and much-loved teacher. When mental loss took away his facility with words, he sometimes descended into discouragement or fear. At those times, I'd remind him that even though he could no longer teach using language, he was still a teacher by virtue of *how* he was living with Alzheimer's. Friends and family validated that. They were inspired and heartened by how he was handling the illness.

This can be true for any of us. Think of friends who have met a difficult illness with courage, who have grown through adversity, who have inspired others. Here is where hope lies. When adversity comes, we can support and inspire each other in countless ways. Sometimes the most valuable gifts we can give—the quality of our presence, for example—are invisible. The truth is that each of us, when faced with a life-threatening illness, is called to the most heroic chapter of our lives.

Without question, Alzheimer's is one of the most difficult of illnesses. It is daunting, tedious, exhausting, financially draining, and heartbreaking: the full catastrophe, as Zorba the Greek referred to life at its most trying. Nor does this disease happen solely to the person who has it; it affects family and friends, which translates into an estimated twenty-nine million Americans who have a family member with the disease. I'm convinced that nearly everyone has been touched—however remotely—by this illness, not only because it is epidemic but because losing one's mind is such a frightening prospect. Currently, estimates claim that there are nearly five million cases of Alzheimer's nationwide; projections declare that by 2050 as many as thirteen to sixteen million people in this country could be suffering with this mythic disease.

The Majesty of Your Loving is a collection of vignettes, reflections, and teachings that intimately reveal how Alzheimer's affects the patient, family, and friends. For the first few years of a six-year journey, Hob was able to offer penetrating and revealing observations about his mental decline. He treated his unraveling mind with playfulness and humor. He even faced death with openness and honesty—another theme in the book which is especially important because ours is a death-denying culture.

To highlight the important insights and learnings of our story, I've added self-help sections at the end of each chapter to encourage you, the reader, to reflect on what may be most helpful. In addition to highlighting main points, each section includes reflections, suggestions, and seed thoughts—simple, prayer-like statements. The seed thoughts are easy to remember and can be used like mantras to refocus and uplift the mind in challenging moments.

The self-help sections include approaches that helped us along the way. Hob and I discovered perspectives and attitudes that lightened the burdens of illness. Determined to live the experience consciously and lovingly, we regarded this—the final challenge of our relationship—as an opportunity for opening to the unknown, for learning, and, above all, for deepening in love.

There were many really hard times, yet, looking back on the experience, it is clear that something precious was forged in the fires of our adversity. This is one of the great mysteries of life: like the metaphors from alchemy where fire transforms one element into another, life's greatest challenges change us forever. When life catapults us into crisis, we touch the archetypal themes of what it really means to be human. This is where the personal and the universal meet.

Our story is everyone's story. Often as I wrote, I felt your presence. It is my deepest hope that you will discover some of the comforting and inspiring themes that sustained us through the most challenging, and richest, chapter of our lives.

CHAPTER ONE

THE ARROW OF SHOCK

We had worked out a good plan, or so I thought at the time. Since we were leaving from disparate points, we needed to take separate cars. I had plotted each step, and even though Hob had made this trip countless times from our home in Cambridge, I wrote out careful instructions. He reassured me that of course he understood the plan. But, just to cover all possible contingencies, I left a detailed note on the seat of his car. We were to meet at a halfway point and then, driving in tandem, proceed together to our family vacation place in Vermont.

The moment I arrived at our rendezvous, a restaurant on the southern border of Vermont, I experienced both relief at being only slightly late and concern that I didn't see Hob's car. He was sometimes late, I reminded myself. But there was a new piece in the puzzle: the year before he had been tentatively diagnosed with Alzheimer's disease.

I ordered lunch, settled down with a newspaper, talked with the waiter, and glanced up every time the door swung open, fully expecting Hob to walk in.

An hour passed. An hour and fifteen minutes.

I was calm, even happy with this unexpected gift of time. *How long should I wait?* I wondered. *Maybe he left late. He always has trouble leaving—a lover of home and place. This is an old, beleaguered issue between us. I'm the one eager to get on our way, while he finds last-minute tasks to delay us. Why hasn't he called? I even gave him the number of the restaurant just in case . . .*

An hour and a half. Now, somewhat alarmed, I went to the phone and called our house in Vermont. Perhaps he forgot and went there. No answer. I sat by the phone, uncertain. Should I call the state police? What if there has been an accident? More dramatic thoughts streamed through my mind.

Alarmist. Extremist. Ridiculous. But what is it going to be like when he's gone? To live without him? This is my buddy, my husband, my lover and companion in life for thirty-three years. What if it's happened this afternoon? The end? Finished? Mightn't anyone be thinking such thoughts at a moment like this?

Still, I remained calm and aware that I was experiencing my thoughts and feelings, and watching them at the same time. Suddenly the manager appeared beside me. "There's a phone call for you."

The moment I picked up the receiver, Hob erupted at the other end of the line. "What happened to me? I couldn't find the exit. Where is White River Junction? I'm in Randolph. I had a terrible time getting the phone number of Howard Johnson's. The operator kept telling me no one by that name lived in White River Junction. What happened?"

I heard the distress in his voice. I'd waited over an hour

and a half, but I felt no anger. How could I? He was telling me that he couldn't find White River Junction—a place we'd driven through hundreds of times. Still, I found it hard to accept that this had happened. If he'd missed the exit, why hadn't he turned around and come back? What about all those U-turn places and other exits? No, he had proceeded to the most familiar place. He had gone to Randolph, a town forty minutes north of White River Junction, which was the exit where we usually turned off to follow the winding back roads to our Vermont house. Of course. On some level it made sense to proceed to "our exit," the familiar place, but, clearly, he'd lost the ability to follow a simple plan. No matter that he'd had forty minutes of driving beyond our meeting point to figure out his mistake. No matter that I had placed the note on the front seat of his car so he wouldn't misplace it. How could I have anticipated he would take the paper into the house, so that, as he said, "I would know where it was," then couldn't find it. Now he was upset and confused, unable even to understand what had gone wrong.

The facts of the situation broke over me like waves too threatening to ride. I tried to sense his level of disorientation, absorb his feelings of dismay. He didn't apologize, or ask how long I'd been waiting, or even say he'd spaced out—all the things you'd expect under normal circumstances. But we were no longer living under "normal circumstances."

"It's okay," I replied, knowing that the most important response was to downplay the situation and be calm for both of us. "I'll drive up to Randolph while you get some lunch. Not to worry. I'll be there in about forty minutes."

As I walked out into the brilliant October afternoon, I became aware of the tangle of intensity in my gut, of the dissonance between the radiance of the day and the distress in my body.

I should have Scotch-taped the yellow paper onto the dashboard and made a back-up copy for him to misplace. . . . Ridiculous! You can't live that way! Face it: another piece of his connection to the physical plane has slipped away. Let it go. Accept that this is just the way things are now.

Meanwhile, how was I to balance the intensity of my feelings with all those yogic teachings I'd practiced over the years? Where was my effort supposed to be in this moment where mind and feelings were embattled? I felt like an animal wounded by an invisible arrow, but I couldn't find the place where it had hit.

I drove away, struggling with my feelings while the inner dialogue raced on. *Look into the face of what's happening. He's losing his ability to handle the practical things we take for granted. There's nothing to hold on to now. No certainties anymore. Feel the fear and sadness. You've got to be a warrior. This is really hard, but you know how to deal with this.*

There were no tears, only the dry catching of my breath. I was okay somewhere, I knew, even as I struggled with the enormity of this one small event in our lives. After all, it was a beautiful afternoon and a spectacular drive.

Several months before, Hob and I were walking down the wide, impersonal hallway of a suburban psychiatric hospital near our home in Cambridge. Earlier that year, he had completed a battery of tests which he had found insufferable.

"They were all set up to trick me," he had said, maybe with some premonition of what lay ahead. "I know I messed up because I was thoroughly irritated with the whole thing."

As we walked into the consulting room for a meeting with the doctor who had ordered the tests, I was struck by the orderliness of the room. Several tables along the walls were covered with articles and printouts, all meticulously laid out in symmetrical piles. The mauve-covered chairs were arranged in a neat circle in preparation for our meeting, and the sunny corner room looked out to the spacious, park-like grounds of the hospital. Although everything about the room was bright and in order, I felt unsettled by a distant dread. I wouldn't let this situation get to me, I reassured myself. Straightening to my full height of five feet, ten inches, and, in a familiar pattern of soldiering through difficult situations, I marshaled all the forces of steadiness and strength that I could summon for this meeting.

Hob wandered toward the window and stood quietly. He commented on the starkness of a dead tree silhouetted against the sky and wondered aloud why, in such beautifully kept grounds, they didn't cut it down. As for what he might be feeling about this meeting, I had no idea. His expression was inscrutable.

At that moment, the doctor strode into the room followed by the social worker, Deborah, to whom we were introduced. The doctor was known for his expertise. We had heard him speak at a public gathering and had met with him once before. Now he reached out to shake our hands in greeting. He motioned for us to sit and began to talk about the test results and what some of the individual tests had shown.

"It's still too early to know anything for sure," he said, "but there was a debate between the two radiologists who looked at the results of the CAT scan and MRI. One thought that there were clearly signs of early Alzheimer's disease, but the second radiologist wasn't so sure. And as you may know, there still isn't any definitive diagnosis when it comes to this disease. There are only the indicators that some process is going on in the brain, and that's what we need to address."

As he continued to talk about protocols and experimental drug trials, I began to feel numb, as if suspended in a distorted sense of time and place where everything seemed distant, as if I were awake in a dream. I glanced at Hob. He still had that masked expression, but the lines in his face seemed etched more deeply than usual—a sign of concern and inner struggle that I recognized after so many years together.

"Well, that's not exactly the cheeriest news to get on a morning like this," my husband said. "Not what I expected."

During a pause in the conversation when the doctor got up to get something from one of the tables, Deborah leaned toward me. I noticed how the sunlight brightened the wavy, reddish-blond hair that framed her open, friendly face. I suddenly felt that she was an island of warmth in the midst of this cool, clinical meeting. She extended her left hand slightly in a gesture of handing the conversation to me.

"How are you doing with all of this?" she asked. "It must be hard for you."

"Yeah, it is very hard. It's a shock even though I suspected something was wrong. Thanks for asking," I replied, but I certainly wasn't going to say anything more in that moment. I would have fallen apart. Her kindness had broken through my armored coping. I felt emotional pain twisting at my heart and gut. My eyes filled with tears, but I refused to let my vulnerability show either to the doctor, whose cool professionalism repelled the realm of feeling, or to Hob, at least in that moment, in that place. I knew Deborah saw and understood—two women sensitive to the deeper feelings that flow at such times. I felt grateful to her for eliciting the one personal moment during the whole consultation.

The meeting came to an end. Hob and I walked back down the hall, both of us quiet, reflecting on what had just happened. I knew this was one of those pivotal moments in life, that I'd been catapulted unexpectedly into a new world where the very ground of things had shifted. There was no going back and I had no idea what lay ahead. I was no longer seeing the world as I had just moments earlier.

We reached the door and started down the steps that led away from the clinic. Out of the silence, Hob spoke. "I don't want to rail against what everyone will experience sooner or later."

I was struck by the tone of acceptance in his voice about his diagnosis. *Our diagnosis*, I thought to myself, knowing instantly the implications for both of us. Hob was only seventy-two, while I was fourteen years younger. Living with that age difference, I had always assumed he would predecease me. Still, no one is ever ready for a catastrophic diagnosis.

In a gesture of comfort, we reached for each other's hands. We are in this one together, I thought, as we walked along the path away from the clinic toward the next, and last, chapter of our lives.

My mother, who had died five years earlier, had also had Alzheimer's. Her saga with the disease had been a complicated and difficult one. I reassured myself that with Hob, the experience would be different. Fragments of thought streamed through my mind. *So many things are different for us: his wit and sense of humor—his primary ways of responding to the world; his playfulness with words; our commitment to honesty and directness in our relationship; our years of studying the nature of the mind through psychology and Buddhist meditation; our spiritual orientation to life—even though he invariably bridled at words like "spiritual"—for that was the bond that originally brought us together.*

Surely all these threads would help us to negotiate whatever lay ahead. They were to become the tapestry of the next six years and the heart of this story: his words, my reflections; his ruminations, my responses; his anxieties, my reassurances; his diminishment, my challenges. We'll walk through this one hand in hand as best we can.

The diagnosis of any life-threatening illness thrusts us into a new dimension. I was intensely aware that we now lived with a third presence—Alzheimer's disease. There was no way to know how it would unfold, for everyone's experience of the disease is unique. For the spouse or family member, there will be a parallel but utterly different experience. I knew that this was going to be a formative—and formidable—journey for both of us. Maybe it was denial, but we had discussions about what attitudes to bring to the disease. Wishing not to accept the usual pathological approach, we would see if we could remain open and curious about an unpredictable journey. Besides surviving, I was determined to reap the benefits, teachings, even perhaps the graces of the disease. And I trusted that our many years of meditation practice would help to sustain us.

After that landmark morning at the diagnostic clinic, I also recognized that we were living with another dimension of time. Something in our midst felt different; we lived with a heightened awareness of what the Greeks called *kairos*, or vertical time, entirely different from *chronos* time, which is linear and familiar. In that verticality, there was a sense of timelessness, sad and sweet. Whether it was the cardinal's arrival at the birdfeeder, the palette of a twilight sky, or the tenderness in Hob's eyes, the littlest moments shimmered with clarity. Life sometimes seemed unbearably precious and precarious.

Then, of course, I would forget. In the early stages—the first couple of years—our lives went on as before. I was teaching, counseling, and writing. Hob was still teaching his classes in Buddhist meditation, although he was more preoccupied over preparing for them than he used to be. He was also still driving and, for the most part, managing his affairs. But there was an accelerating succession of little indicators: the names forgotten, the errant word, the lost keys, the touching exchange. Life may be woven of ordinary moments, yet increasingly, poignancy or grief or humor intensified the quality of our life together.

Hob had always had a penchant for playing with words. He had majored in English, received a PhD in Comparative Literature, and taught most of his life. His love of language was a continual source of delight and wit for him and everyone around him. Hard as it was to watch his "word hoard," as he called it, growing smaller, his playfulness with language was to be a blessing. He often transformed the frustration of the moment into a funny expression, a game with words, or a pun.

"I get betrayed by colors!" he would say, laughing, as he tried to find something. He'd refer to "the wily trickster of the physical plane," his expression for describing his increasingly perilous relationship with the material world. Things disappeared. Familiar objects weren't in drawers. Carefully crafted lists dematerialized off his desk. "I'm always being tricked by things. Grab on to whatever stick of kindling you can when you're going down with the Titanic," he declared with a laugh.

He turned to humor and poetry as lifelines to a fading

world. One early morning during the winter after his diagnosis, he stood by the bedroom window looking out at the stately elm beside the house, now covered with several inches of newly fallen snow. The morning was dark with the heavy cloud cover of the departing storm. For someone who was almost unfailingly cheerful first thing in the morning, he seemed as somber as the weather. He turned toward me with a furrowed expression.

"I can't get it. Just fragments are there. Here, sit with me on the bed until I can find the rest," he said, as we sat down together in the half-light.

"Can you remember anything about what the subject is?" I asked. "Something that happened yesterday, or . . ."

"I'm not sure it's articulable," he began and then paused. "It's inarticulable. It's a poem, part of a sonnet that Milton wrote to his recently departed wife. Like the feel of this morning, all in a few lines. I remember that much. It drives me crazy not to be able to come up with something I know so well. It's about his dream. He could only see her in his dream.

"'So happy but I waked'—there's one line . . . I think it's coming back."

Another long silence while I slipped into the familiar practice of waiting. I could feel his struggle to remember something treasured that was now irretrievable. It seemed so urgent. With every loss, one more symbolic sinking. These slow, attenuated exchanges had become more frequent. I felt a surge of impatience, then realized that the problem wasn't a need to hurry but my own grief at his growing disability. Impatience was easier to deal with than feeling the depth of my grief.

Then Hob began to squeeze my hand in rhythm with the lines as he recited them.

> **I dreamed I saw my late departed wife,**
> **So happy but I waked, she fled,**
> **And day brought back my night.**[1]

"There, that's it!" he exclaimed, as if he'd just discovered a lost treasure. "You can't imagine what this is like," he continued. "Those words express something I could never say as well, but they elude me. I get consternated. I'm sorry." He turned to me, his expression forlorn again.

"I actually had the chutzpah to think I could beat the rap—beat this diagnosis—but this morning it doesn't look that way," he said. "Now it's about finding out how many fire escapes there are in a building. I don't know where to find the help I need. It's like being condemned to death by hanging and then going around looking for someone who fixes sore throats."

Heavy as the subject was, he began to laugh at his own image.

"Now that's a good one! Don't know where that came from." And he turned to hug me as if to celebrate that some great weight had been lifted from his shoulders.

The exchange that morning epitomized how life with Hob had taken on a precipitous, even vertiginous quality. I never knew what the next loss or shock might be. I was stunned by the fluctuations in his states. At times, he was so articulate I'd forget that anything was wrong. Other times, his faltering words reverberated between us, leaving a vacuum. Parts of him seemed to have disappeared. One minute almost his old self; the next an old man, dreamy and disconnected, moving slowly as if under water. I felt caught between the two realities. There was the enduring sense of the person I'd always known—vivid, engaged, and amusing—but then the new reality would break over me in waves. Sometimes the waves were small and mildly breath-catching; other times they threatened to tumble me into a chaos of overwhelming feelings.

Most of us, most of the time, rest complacently in the illusion that our lives have some measure of stability. In reality, we all live on the edge of the unknown. "Maybe even on the edge of an abyss," an older friend once remarked to me, wryly. Something about the nature of Hob's illness finally drove home that stark truth.

More frequently now, his expression collapsed into flatness. His eyes were dull, his demeanor almost that of a dead man walking. Where was his former spark of life? The animation? The connection? Who was he now? A succession of questions gathered on the edge of my awareness.

As a result of never knowing where he might be on this dramatic continuum, I discovered a new dimension of mindfulness: gentle vigilance. Mindfulness—also described as moment-to-moment awareness—is a simple but powerful approach to life that lies at the heart of Buddhist practice. I purposefully invoked openness and flexibility. I cultivated equanimity. In this new, unpredictable world where I often felt as if I were walking into gale force winds, I leaned into the moment, fiercely awake, ready for anything.

After a series of unnerving episodes, I evolved a ritual for coming home, even if I'd been away for only a few hours. I thought of it as my "pathway practice," not something I'd heard in a dharma talk (a Buddhist teaching talk) or read in a book, but a spontaneous practice that arose in response to a difficult situation. Each time I arrived home, in those moments between leaving the car, stepping onto the old brick walk, and entering the house, I shifted into mindfulness practice: walking and breathing mindfully, aware of each step, each breath. Just before the door, I repeated a simple *metta* or loving-kindness prayer. That was how I steadied myself in preparation for the inevitable—the latest crisis waiting for me on the other side of the door.

"I can't find my date-book, and I think I have an appointment now."

"Someone's urgently trying to reach you, but I can't find my note for you."

"When you're gone, I feel this melancholy creeping over me and I have catastrophic fantasies that something's happened to you."

I'd feel the chains of responsibility tightening. How could I leave the house every day? How could I sustain my own life, apart from this caretaking? How would I survive the intensity of his feelings—the urgency, even desperation, behind his questions?

I wondered about the ruthlessness of his swings. Did he experience them, too, or was he protected by some diminishment in awareness? What did he experience when the blankness descended? One of my Buddhist teachers asked me during a meditation retreat if I could simply observe what happened to Hob's awareness in the course of the disease. I knew from his compassionate inquiry that he was also declaring himself an ally in our journey, a support for me. He had once spoken of his own fears of dementia, a fear which probably every one of us carries.

Because of my passionate wish to understand what Hob was experiencing, I questioned him frequently. "Where are you?" or "What's going on?" or "Can you tell me what you're experiencing right now?" His answers were usually vague.

"Oh, just dreaming." Or, because he sensed my concern, he would pull up some practical response, such as, "Just thinking the gutters need to be cleaned."

Was it hard for him? Or was he blessedly suspended in some *bardo*-like state, some in-between moment, like a sailboat in irons adrift because, momentarily, there is no wind in its sails? (In the Tibetan tradition, the term *bardo* refers to any in-between moment, especially passing from life into death and beyond.) Determined to remain steady, I responded to each latest crisis. I soldiered on as if nothing had changed from the last thirty-four years of our lives together. Yet I knew in my heart that more often he was drifting away into inaccessible realms. Like sound disappearing into the distance, his vibrant, engaged self was vanishing, ever more diffuse, ever more remote.

━━ ∞ ━━

When we first learned of Hob's diagnosis, we discussed how our years of Buddhist practice could help us navigate whatever lay ahead. We saw that Buddhist teachings were a container to hold the shifting realities of disease, that they could offer a helpful perspective as well as inspiration. All of us know, at some level, that we will face aging, dying, and death, but our youth-oriented culture is steeped in denial and phobic about these topics. Hob and I refused to collude in this denial. Rather, we were determined to face directly into what was happening. We talked about it regularly. And he was unusual both in his openness about having the disease and in his attitude toward death.

"Fools! Would you live forever?" he would declare with theatrical flair, quoting the words of some general exhorting his troops to go fearlessly into battle, fearless even of death.

For me, there was an added incentive to face this challenge. In the case of my mother, our family's experience, and surely hers, was complicated by lack of knowledge about Alzheimer's as well as by her inability to speak about it.

I was determined to do everything I could to enable Hob to live his last years with more ease than my mother had. Part of that decision was to seek new perspectives wherever I could

21

find them.

One of my first steps was to call upon Tulku Thondup, a Tibetan teacher whom I had met years earlier when I first began looking for a meditation teacher. As I was then very new to Buddhist teachings, it was a memorable meeting. Tulku Thondup, also known as T.T., had talked about the law of impermanence in a quiet, compelling way. His words about this core teaching of the Buddha stayed with me, like a wisdom treasure to which I could turn whenever I remembered. Periodically, I would call upon him, especially when I was going through difficult times and needed a more spacious perspective. He became a spiritual friend—a *kalyana mitta*—that beautiful term from the Buddhist tradition that describes a special relationship with someone who supports and inspires one's inner life.

One brilliant, windy October morning, I was on my way once again to meet with T.T. He lived on a quiet side street in my neighborhood, and as I walked, watching leaves dance along the pavement, I was preoccupied with the increasing challenges of Hob's disease. I wanted to ask him how Tibetans look upon dementia, how they care for their elders, and what approaches from the Buddhist teachings might help us.

He welcomed me to his small apartment and brought out green tea in blue and white mugs that had little lids to keep the tea warm.

He settled into his wingback chair. Like many Tibetans he seemed ageless, his presence both gentle and strong. As I spoke, he listened, his expression serene, the hint of a smile softening his face. Then he began to speak in a stream of observations that seemed to flow effortlessly from a deep source.

"You and Hob have common karma," he told me. "Take it as a blessing. Any situation can be a source of growth. This is difficult, but it is a teaching, a training, a blessing. And so you should try to use it as much as you can. You should feel very fortunate for what you have; feel gratitude for all the blessings of your life. See them. Feel them. Then this whole situation becomes a healing process. Why worry? Whatever we do for each other and for others will be an improvement, will be a healing of this life.

"Taking care of him will become a meditation for you, a practice. Meditation, as you know, creates many good merits. It may not be visible to others, but our helping each other is a merit-making process. If you need to help him, you will be practicing the six perfections (patience, generosity, discipline, diligence, contemplation, and wisdom). This is the most important practice. Even giving a mouthful of food could include all these perfections. Maybe some hardship will be involved, but then you cultivate patience."

I realized that he was explaining how the simplest activity of helping can be a practice, a way to reframe difficulties and cultivate helpful qualities. He went on.

"Whatever you do to help, do it with total concentration. The wisdom in this case would be the wisdom of non-self, giving as a dedication, as a service to others, with no attachment or grasping. Do whatever you do joyfully, because discipline—the true meaning of the word—is characterized by doing something with joy. Even the little things: see them as an opportunity, a blessing, a meditation, as spiritual practice. Then, even if it's difficult, it will be good. If you use hardships in a proper way, they can even bring inner peace."

"What about in Tibet?" I asked. "How do people regard dementia there? How do families handle it?"

"Of course, many older people get dementia, but it's not seen as something so unusual, like here," T.T. said. "Families usually live in villages or in some community where there are many people in the extended family to help. Someone can wander around and it's okay. If it's a lama or someone who has done a lot of practice, they assume that they are in high states even if they seem crazy or in strange mind-states."

I was struck by his last point. In his culture the dissembling of the mind is looked upon as a natural process, like the dissembling of the body. Both are in the natural order of things. Because community and extended family remain strong forces in society, the elders remain in community. Caregiving is shared by many more family and friends than we have in our nuclear models of living.

"Remember," T.T. continued, "we can reframe our attitude toward pain. It can even be good, because whenever you are in pain, you know you are burning past bad karmas. When problems come to you, try not to see them as negative. They are a part of life, like day and night, day and night. It's not day, day, day. Use negative situations positively, and they can all become a helpful source of benefit—even if they are painful. Pain is the most powerful tool of meditation. In the human plane there is so much turmoil, and that means this is a place for practice. Use the problems in your life as incentives for growth; then they become a blessing, not a curse.

"Human life is so blessed," he continued. "We are blessed because we know of so many ways to deal with these challenges. Our experiences are always teaching us. You can be tortured or worshiped or peaceful—all in one life."

I assumed he was referring to the pervasive suffering that the Tibetans have endured since the Chinese invasions. I knew that he had fled the country, lost family members, suffered as an exile, his earlier life destroyed. He continued.

"So problems remind us to practice. And the most important thing is to prepare for our death. All of our practices, especially meditation, are a preparation for death. So you end up turning life into practice—that is what we want to do. With meditation, you develop peace and strength. They are the same, like synonyms: if you're peaceful, you have strength; if you have strength, you have peace. True strength is when someone is calm, peaceful, without worries.

"Acknowledge the peacefulness in yourself—see it, feel it, believe in it. By cultivating a positive quality like peace, compassion, or any other quality, you use the power of belief to enhance that quality in you. These positive qualities are always present. You realize them by recollection, by remembering, by waking up."

He paused, and then said, "Remember also that the wise ones are a source of protection and blessings which you can call on. At night when you prepare to sleep, bring the visualization of them into your heart and you will receive protection and blessings through the night."

His perspective, born of his culture and training, created space around the difficulties of my life. His quiet assurance made anything seem possible. I felt supported in my determination to approach Hob's dementia with the wisdom of the dharma, the classic teachings. They would help us to meet whatever lay ahead.

The visit had given me some helpful perspectives, but it had also stirred memories of my mother's experience with Alzheimer's. Her situation had been complicated by a family doctor who failed to diagnose her spiraling into psychosis in addition to Alzheimer's. Our family stood helplessly by as she descended into crazed states, crying out for unending hours, calling for connection and for help that she wasn't getting. During one period that lasted several days, she repeated over and over with terrible urgency, "The people who are tortured, the people who are tortured, the people who are tortured . . ." This phrase must have been about her own suffering, but was she also feeling the pain of the world as well? We would never know.

My mother had been swept into a vortex of madness so powerful that she became temporarily blind. We thought the blindness was permanent—another ruthless symptom of disease. But it turned out that the blindness was part of an undiagnosed psychosis that had compounded the Alzheimer's.

We found a skilled psychiatrist, moved her to a nursing home, and miraculously, it seemed to us, the psychosis lifted. She experienced a remarkable comeback, including the return of her vision. She even came home for a couple of nights each week as we tried to rebuild a familiar life around her.

Now that she was elderly and suffering, I wanted to reach through the barriers of her disease. What was she experiencing? How did she feel as she sat there, increasingly cut off from her intellect? She, who had been a writer and poet. After her language had fallen away completely, I used to think that my mother might be in an inner state that we couldn't fathom. Her brain might be compromised by disease, but what of the consciousness that is beyond the rational mind? Could she have been in some state of pure being, free from suffering because there was no mind to analyze what was happening to her? I used to think that perhaps she was hanging out in "the cave of the heart," a phrase from the yogic traditions that I loved. That perhaps she was doing some kind of inner work we couldn't imagine. How could we know? There were times when she was agitated, but there were many times when she seemed serene, deeply peaceful.

Even if these intuitions were rationalization on my part, they gave me comfort. Because who knew for sure? No one. Not the nurses or social workers, not the Alzheimer's professionals or doctors. There is no way to measure "soul work," and I intu-ited that sometimes my mother was doing exactly that—soul work—in realms of consciousness beyond our knowing.

One afternoon, we were sitting in the courtyard of the nurs-ing home. She sat in her wheelchair; I was on a bench next to her. She was looking at me with unusual intensity, as if on the edge of words. Suddenly, looking straight at me with those bril-liant blue eyes, the words exploded out of her with great force.

"God, physics, and the cosmos!"

I took a deep breath to steady myself.

"What extraordinary words, Ma!" I said, finally. "What a message! You're telling me—and I can only guess—that there is some mysterious connection between these things—God, phys-ics, and the cosmos." I purposely repeated her words slowly and clearly, turning them for her like treasures.

The faintest smile softened her flat expression. We remained in silence. Her words became a koan for me. A koan is a riddle intended to awaken the mind to its inherent nature, and while someone else might have interpreted her words as nonsense, knowing my mother's inquiring, philosophical mind, they lingered: a gift, an intimation, perhaps, of something indecipherable by the left brain, by ordinary mind.

Tibetan teachers speak of "the twilight language," a secret code of Tantric terminology which refers to language that can't be understood by the left hemisphere of the brain. Was my mother speaking in a twilight language that could only be received through a liminal process of knowing—open, receptive, intuitive? In what inner spaces did she dwell that gave rise to such a statement? Did her words point to some mystery that she had been pondering, even if in a limited way? Perhaps she was like a retreatant living in her own inner cave, far from us all, yet not without some inner process that was helping her negotiate the uncharted territory of losing ordinary mind.

Without denying the enormity of what she was living through, I occasionally wondered if we, her family, were suffering more than she was.

⁘ ⟐ ⁘

"If this just weren't all a little bit funny, it wouldn't be very pleasant." Those were Hob's words as he came downstairs for breakfast one morning after a rocky beginning to the day: a lost razor, an errant shirt, a missing word.

He sat down at the dining table in our family room and lapsed into silence, absorbed in thought as he gazed out at the garden. During the night, the first gentle snowfall of early winter had brushed the garden with white, and the room was brilliant with the morning sun reflecting off the snow.

Hob turned back toward me and continued. "If you want to be entertained by your own downfall, better to do it knowingly than get all choked up by the inevitable. I can feel the slipping; it's like having quicksand under me. Sometimes if I don't say something right away, it's like a wild bird. It's gone. It's delicate, this business of memory and words."

He was still remarkably lucid about describing what he

was going through. In fact, that was part of our agreement. In our discussions about how we would handle the challenges of Alzheimer's, we had gone back over my mother's experience and determined, if possible, to do things differently. One never knows how an illness will unfold, especially brain disease. Still, we had several clear intentions.

Our years of meditation practice—which develops increasing awareness about the nature of the mind—impelled us to stay in close touch over what he was experiencing. What was happening to his mind? In what areas were the losses coming? Could he describe how it felt?

"Please keep me posted with these reports from the interior, no matter what they are," I said to him one day. "I want to know what's going on. I'll write down as much as I can, because maybe it will be helpful for other people going through this."

Sometimes he would turn to me and ask, What are you seeing? Will you tell me sometimes what this is like from your perspective?"

This was fairly easy in the early stages, but later on it became complicated; I wanted to affirm his remaining abilities, not focus on his losses. He had enough to deal with without having me do that. Nevertheless, in our early conversations we made a commitment to live openly with the process. As I said over and over again to friends when explaining the situation, we wanted to live this as consciously and lovingly as possible. *Consciously and lovingly* became my inner compass pointing to magnetic north.

REFLECTIONS, SUGGESTIONS, AND SEED THOUGHTS

As mentioned in the Introduction, I have included a section at the end of each chapter to highlight psychological and spiritual perspectives that may illuminate the process of caring for someone with dementia. A set of reflections, suggestions, and seed thoughts—simple, prayer-like statements—are also included to frame the section and make the material more accessible to you. My hope is that these guidelines will remind you of the teachings that are woven through the book and encourage you to find your own way of adapting them to your situation. I wrote these sections to serve as both companion and guide because we are bonded through the shared experience of dealing with this great challenge.

DIAGNOSIS AND BEYOND
Reflections

* One of the most critical moments in life is learning that one has a life-threatening illness. Whether you are the patient, spouse, family member, or friend, acknowledge the enormity of receiving this news and the time it takes to integrate the new reality into one's life.

* Accept that the diagnosis, with all its implications, will have a profound impact on your marriage, relationship, or friendship. A diagnosis of Alzheimer's, or any form of dementia, marks a dramatic passage for everyone and naturally brings up strong, unpredictable feelings.

* Understand how natural it is for a wide range of feelings to arise: numbness, denial, sadness, dread, despair, fear, grief, anger, and so on. Each of us has different ways of handling our feelings, but we care for our health and well-being when we open to their intensity. Be gentle and nonjudgmental with yourself, your spouse, and others when strong feelings arise; acceptance is a gradual process.

* Remember that as well as being a journey of loss, this is also an opportunity for learning and growth. When I first heard Tulku Thondup say, "take it as a blessing," I struggled with those words. How could he possibly say that? What was he getting at? Upon reflection, I knew he intended it as an invitation to see the opportunities in our situation, and that he was framing it in the most uplifting, spacious way possible. Whenever I remembered that phrase, my perspective on our situation expanded. I felt both challenged and hopeful. I knew I would be learning life's hardest lessons: loss, surrender, dying, and death. And along

with these was the opportunity to deepen in trust and love.

Suggestions

* Who can you turn to for support? Consider sitting down with your spouse, family members, or trusted friends and brainstorm what your resources are: supportive family members, friends, minister or rabbi, therapist, financial advisor, and so forth. Find out what Alzheimer's resources there are in your area: an Alzheimer's center, support groups, adult day programs for the future. Check out the Internet for further information. See the Selected Bibliography at the end of this book. Read about Rehabilitation Therapy, a practical program for dementia patients that suggests many effective strategies for handling this disease.

* Develop a care plan for the immediate future—perhaps the first six months—because with this illness, circumstances keep changing and the care plan will need to evolve in response. Create a plan that addresses the physical, emotional, social, and spiritual needs of the patient.

Besides the practical advantages of developing a care plan, you can have a strategic discussion about how you hope to handle this illness. What hopes, attitudes, and convictions might you bring to the situation? Are there intentions you could set? Two words that guided us were *consciously and lovingly*. What words or phrases might inspire and comfort you? For example: kindness, openness, caring, tenderness, patience, acceptance, compassion, and so on.

＊ Is there any one person who stands out for you who might be an ally for you? This person might be a family member, friend, wise elder, minister, rabbi, or teacher.

＊ Start practicing ways to steady yourself by cultivating calmness in difficult moments. In those times, become aware of your body and your breath. Practice noticing how several deep, calming breaths can steady you. An invaluable practice in any situation is to keep returning to the rhythm of your breath to anchor you to the present moment.

Seed Thoughts

May I accept the challenges of this situation.

May I be gentle with myself.

Let me be calm.
(Or cultivate whatever quality you most need:
patience, equanimity, kindness, compassion.)

CHAPTER TWO

THE GRACE OF DIMINISHMENT

In keeping with our agreement to communicate openly about the experience of mental loss, Hob would often make insightful observations about his own mind. Each one was like a treasure, or sometimes a landmine depending on what he'd brought forth; but either way, his insights revealed the awareness that so far continued to be there.

"They're all here—the perceptions, ideas, and inspirations. They come in as before, but now they seem more fleeting. They're here, vivid, ready to express, but like a prairie dog, suddenly they disappear down the hole and they're gone. This is what it's like now—fleeting experiences of mind. Now it's here. Now it's gone."

What a powerful teaching on the impermanence of mind, thoughts, any solid sense of self! His thoughts, he said, were like traces on a radar screen. Some of them made strong, emotional marks, whereas others just floated through, leaving scarcely a trace. Some of those fleeting thoughts kicked up a strong reaction; others were like gossamer or milkweed on the wind—here, then suddenly gone.

"Isn't it something, the way things walk out of you!" he exclaimed one day, expressing wonder toward the process he was living through.

Sometimes this play of the mind wasn't a matter of wonder at all, but deeply unsettling. Two critical times of day were when Hob awoke in the morning and after he awoke from an afternoon nap. Most of us take for granted the easy transition from one state of consciousness to another, from sleeping to waking. Not so when the mind is impaired.

"When I've woken up these last few days, there's been no one home. The blackboard is erased. You're supposed to be able to pick up where you left off—to remember something. But there's nothing. You wake up and you don't know where you're going today or what you're supposed to be doing; it's very unsettling. I want to be able to teach, to remember enough to do that. But I can't remember the ideas I had yesterday. All erased. It feels like a defeat."

I began to notice how often Hob used words to find his way back to some semblance of mental order. He, the former professor of English, the dharma teacher, loved words. In fact, words were his world: he loved playing with them; he delighted himself and others with how he used words. What would happen when the words were gone? I'd catch myself in that imponderable, dead-end thought.

After all, in the year after his diagnosis he was still teaching, and we were teaching a class together. The subject of our class was "meditation and conscious aging." He had been very open with the class about his situation, and that had created riveting moments for everyone. Even though I was carrying primary responsibility for it, I knew that the course had stirred up a lot of uncertainty for him.

"I've got to get used to this thrashing around," he said. "I don't know what I know anymore, and if what I think I know will be there tomorrow. What I know is apt to be on extended holiday." He laughed at the image.

"Anyway, it's depressing not to have anything for sure, but I know I need to get over the fear of not knowing the words."

For him, that must have been an incomprehensible challenge.

For me, I wondered what lay ahead. At the same time, bright fragments of our early history together flashed into my mind.

Balancing a glass of wine in one hand and an hors d'oeuvre in the other, I carefully sat down on the couch, mainly to get out of the way of the cluster of people gathered at the kitchen counter. Eight people, mostly unknown to one another, had gathered for a dinner party at this small New York City apartment. It was the spring of 1963, still early in the momentous decade of the sixties. The apartment belonged to Jane, an acquaintance I hardly knew, and in the awkward, early moments of the evening I almost wished that I hadn't come at all. I didn't know anyone. The room felt crowded. In truth, my mind was elsewhere.

I took a long sip of wine and watched as an older man

in a tailored suit approached the couch and settled down beside me. I didn't look at him directly but rather at his hands. He had beautiful hands, deeply tanned with long, tapered fingers. Maybe the hands of an artist or a musician, I thought to myself. In something of a statement, or maybe an understatement, his tie was attached to his shirt with a paperclip, a surprising detail given his otherwise impeccable appearance. He turned toward me, and with the beginnings of a smile, he said, "So tell me what you're up to in your life these days—not just the ordinary things but what's unusual—challenging perhaps. I'm Harrison Hoblitzelle—the name's Swiss German—but everyone calls me Hob." He touched my hand lightly to make contact, not to shake hands.

I was startled by this unusual introduction. Who was this man with his bold invitation to conversation? He was of medium height with the erect bearing and slender build of someone athletic who spent time in the outdoors. His dark, wavy hair was flecked with gray, as was his carefully trimmed beard, rarely seen on a man in those days. He had an unusually broad, high forehead deeply etched with lifelines, the marks of laughter and sorrow clearly visible. His light blue eyes revealed a surprising combination of detachment, humor, even mischievousness.

As our first conversation continued, I began to see how he was perpetually scanning for the playful possibilities of any subject. He exuded quiet self-assurance and was obviously an intellectual. I learned that he was forty years old, fourteen years my elder, and still a bachelor. For me, a much younger woman, there was something opaque and intriguing about him. What had he experienced? What was he hiding behind that detached, nimble-witted, merry demeanor? I felt so much younger and scrambled to keep up with him.

At least I knew I'd dressed well for the occasion! For the first time I was wearing a dress that had been made for me—at my mother's insistence. Usually I wandered around the basements of department stores in search of bargains. The three-quarter length dress, with its classic design, was made of silk in an exquisite shade of moss green. It made me feel elegant and sophisticated. Pinned just below my neck was my favorite piece of jewelry—a strikingly large, delicately wrought, gold-filigreed bridal pendant that had come to me from my Danish grandmother. I had inherited the Nordic look—tall, blond, and blue-eyed—and was proud of my Danish heritage, with which I felt a deep connection.

Somehow it came out in this first conversation that neither Hob nor I had particularly wanted to come to the dinner party. But in that phase of life when one tends to be prowling for a partner, one accepts invitations—even reluctantly—on the chance of meeting someone interesting. At the time, I was still in love with another man and dreaming hopelessly about a relationship that couldn't work out. The wound probably wasn't visible that evening, but I felt guarded as I sat next to this urbane, cosmopolitan man named Hob.

Surprised to find that we were both at Columbia University, we exchanged stories about our lives, laying the ground of fact, but also going deeper with questions and reflections. Hob's thoughtful questions and responses were far from typical of the men I usually went out with. My interest was stirring.

Gradually, pieces of our life portraits began to emerge. Hob came from an old, conservative St. Louis family, but he had clearly turned out to be something of a maverick from that traditional background. After college, he became involved with the Quakers and worked with the social justice activists of that era: A.J. Muste, Bayard Rustin, and Martin Luther King, Jr. among them. He had led many Quaker work camps in Europe and Haiti, he explained, which prompted him to write his thesis on Gandhi and "The War Against War in the 19th Century: The Western Background of Gandhian Thought." He laughed with delight that his topic, given its vast literary scope, had confounded the English department at Columbia where he had done his graduate work.

He was animated and eloquent as he described how much of Gandhi's philosophy came "through the light of Western windows," as he put it. He told me how he had retraced the steps in Gandhi's evolution: how Gandhi had read Emerson and Thoreau, absorbed the social philosophy of Carlyle and Ruskin, and was inspired by Tolstoy's impassioned writing on social issues. His dissertation, Hob explained, cut across four major traditions.

"That's what beleaguered my thesis committee," he said, "but how could it be otherwise if one is intrigued by the intersections between literature and philosophy, peace and social justice work."

As I watched his expressive face, I wondered what lay beneath his self-possessed demeanor. I wouldn't learn until later about his difficult childhood, about an emotionally deprived family life, about his afflictive relationship with his mother, or about the endocrine problem that stunted his growth. When he graduated from boarding school, he was still only five feet two and his voice hadn't changed; at eighteen, he hadn't yet reached puberty—a crucifixion for a teenager.

A few years later, he would contract undulant fever while working in the rain forests of Mexico. With a severe illness complicated by psychological problems including thoughts of suicide, he languished in a hospital. Basically, he lost a year and a half of ordinary life; he'd felt he was a drop-out and a failure because all his friends were going off to war. No wonder that face, deeply etched with lifelines, reflected so much early suffering.

Although I was somewhat daunted by his wide-ranging knowledge, I began to tell parts of my own story. Our backgrounds were similar. I'd grown up mainly on Long Island, received a privileged education, and traveled a fair amount for my years, mainly to Europe and South America. In an effort to break new ground from my heavy New England heritage, I had moved to California after college to work in international relations, then back to Washington, D.C., where I worked for the Peace Corps during the vibrant, idealistic Kennedy era. In an exciting, wonderful job that challenged my limited life experience, I traveled around the country training volunteers for Peace Corps service.

"That's when I discovered I loved to teach," I explained to him. "And so, as crazy as some people might think it was, I left that glamorous job to come here to Columbia to get my master's in history so I can teach at the secondary level."

That's when we found that we both loved teaching. I didn't tell him that night, however, about another stream that ran beneath the surface of my life. I'd always been a dreamer with a secret inner life. As a young girl, I once fantasized that Jesus chose me as his bride, and in a surge of dramatic religiosity, pricked my fingers and made crosses of blood in my Bible. I pondered the eternal questions: Who are we? Why are we here? What is this mystery in which we live? I questioned why people didn't talk more about the wonders of the world—how, for example, plants created flowers, or how there could be an infinity of stars in the night sky, or what caused the phosphorescence in the night waters of Long Island Sound.

I wondered, too, why I was in this body and you were in yours. Why couldn't I get out of my body to feel what it was like to be in yours—to be you? I used to try, but I couldn't make it happen! I simply knew in my young mind that we were part of something larger. That intrigued me. Although I couldn't articulate it then, I intuited that people were in essence spiritual beings, even if they called it by many different names, and that we lived our lives as part of a great mystery

As Hob's and my meandering conversation that first evening

drew to an end, I was both drawn to and puzzled by his detached, bemused outlook on life. Something was stirring for me, but I had no idea where it might lead.

In spite of my early struggle over our age difference, our relationship unfolded very quickly. A few days later when we met for lunch at the Faculty Club—a safe venue for a first date—we talked about the nature of time, religion, and philosophy. Very much the professor even in his way of being with a woman, he recommended that I read *Nature, Man and Woman*, a book by Alan Watts, as if looking for some way for me to catch up to him. Flattered and intrigued, I eagerly read the book. Hob and I soon discovered that we shared not only an interest in psychology and religion, but many other subjects that would sustain our relationship.

We married a year later. Our paths were to overlap in more ways than marriage. As educators, we were to work together at different times through the years. Our first child, Ethan, was born in California where we had gone to help start a school. Our daughter, Laura, was born three years later.

Throughout the permutations of work life, we shared an enduring commitment to teaching. In parallel career shifts, we trained in psychology and the new therapies that were blossoming in the early seventies. That was also the decade when meditation became mainstream. Over the next three decades, we would study with a number of eminent teachers, sometimes following different paths which tested our relationship in new, occasionally stressful ways. In the early nineties, Hob was ordained as a Dharmacharya, or senior teacher, by Thich Nhat Hanh, the Vietnamese Zen master well known for his gift for making the teachings of Buddhism widely available to audiences in the West.

It was in the year before Hob's diagnosis, while he was still teaching classes in Buddhist meditation, that the first signs of trouble emerged. I hardly noticed at first. For one thing, he'd always been something of the absent-minded professor. What was the difference between the accepted memory losses of aging and signs that something more serious could be wrong? We found out that spring day at the diagnostic clinic with the results of the neurological tests. That was when we first heard the word Alzheimer's disease attached to Hob's symptoms.

⸺ ⁓⦵⁓ ⸺

The first of many exchanges that would reveal Hob's way of handling his illness occurred one fall afternoon. It was one of those soft Indian summer days that make one forget that an unpredictable New England winter could strike at any time. We lived in a brown shingled house in Cambridge in a quiet cul-de-sac off a busy street. Originally our house was small and had started out as a rental, but when we were able to buy it, we added on a family room with glass doors and windows on three sides, and opened up the attic. The attic was a beautiful space, like a tree house, which became the guest room and Hob's study. Our house had seen an abundance of good times, plenty of family struggles, and lots of celebrations.

Outside, in the middle of our little circular street, there was an island of grass with several large shade trees, an ideal place for the neighborhood children to play. Our two children, Ethan and Laura, along with the neighboring children, grew up on the circle, amidst a frolicking scene of bicycle races, kid's Olympics, and the predictable skirmishes of kids at play, including an impressive number of broken windows, tokens of wild baseball games and errant slingshots. Our front garden, like all the others, was lined with an old brick sidewalk, heaving and buckling from the expanding roots of the tall trees that lined the circle. In the back of the house, we had a terrace and lawn bordered by shrubs and flowers, at that time of year mainly chrysanthemums and fall asters.

Because our front door had an unreliable old brass lock which never seemed quite broken enough to fix, we used the side door nearer the kitchen. That fall afternoon I was sitting in the living room when I heard the side door open. It was Hob returning from teaching his meditation class. Although it was still only about a year since his diagnosis, I worried and wondered if he'd make it through the remaining weeks of the class. Instantly I knew that something significant had happened, for he walked into the room as if he were carrying something very fragile. He was deeply indrawn and preoccupied.

He came over and sat down beside me on the couch, then reached over, pulled me into a strong hug, and held me for a long time in silence. These were intense, precious moments, both of us hovering at the edge of the unknown—moments for me of radical openness when my mind became totally still, awake and spacious. I never knew what might come next. Finally, he spoke.

"The most amazing thing just happened. . . . I don't know if I can talk about it."

A long pause. I waited for what seemed a long time and then asked, "Can you even point to it—to what happened?"

"It happened in my class. I couldn't remember what I wanted to say to them. It was all gone. But there were the three poems. I knew it was one of them that I wanted. The Yeats poem. I knew it was key, the most important thing. The key to everything. 'A blessing and I could bless.' Those are the words in the poem, at the end. How do you talk about that? Words kill it, but it's all in those words."

"Were you able to remember the poem?"

"Yes. Finally."

He paused again and then began to recite. He savored the words, speaking each one as if it were a treasure.

> My fiftieth year had come and gone,
> I sat, a solitary man,
> In a crowded London shop,
> An open book and empty cup
> On the marble table-top.
> While on the shop and street I gazed
> My body of a sudden blazed;
> And twenty minutes more or less
> It seemed, so great my happiness,
> That I was blessèd and could bless.[1]

Silence. His eyes were soft, filled with tears. I understood then how that poem, one of his favorites, had touched so deep a place. It intimated how the ordinary moment—sitting in a shop, the empty cup, the table top, the street scene—can open into an epiphany.

"That man didn't ask for anything," Hob said. "He wasn't expecting anything. That experience just happened. It was an opening. Everything that I might want to say is in those words 'That I was blessèd and could bless.'"

His eyes held inexpressible feeling: Wonder. Tenderness. Vulnerability.

That poem, other poems, fragments of remembered poetry—these would be Hob's talismans over the few years that remained. His face shining with triumph and delight, he would articulate each line with relish. Through poetry, he was blessed.

Even so, as the weeks and months passed, I increasingly felt a sense of disconnection between us. It was not through lack of communication or understanding, but because of a space that Hob could no longer reliably reach across.

What was it that I saw in his eyes? Not only a deep, pervading fear at times, but a persistent questioning. When I walked into the kitchen one afternoon, I experienced one of those moments of suddenly seeing him with new eyes. He was so different in appearance and energy from a year ago. An image arose: Hob was fading, like an old photograph that had been exposed to incessant light until time renders the image almost indistinguishable. He seemed frail now, an old man, detached from the physical plane, with those eyes that seemed to ask, "What am I doing here? What am I supposed to be doing now?"

At moments, it felt to me as if no one was home, as if part of his soul was already wandering, suspended somewhere in space. He seemed detached from his body. Gone was the instant connection we'd feel when meeting at the end of the day. Was it easier for him to float free rather than be here? Was he thinking about anything or just being? But it wasn't "just being." *Just being* suggested full presence, engagement in the moment. Often I found myself asking such questions for him. I tried to fathom the depths—or was it the shallows—of his experience.

During these tender exchanges, I'd notice that my body was tight with grief and unshed tears. Then I heard the invitation from within myself: *Let go. It's all right to feel the grief.* Grief opens the heart of compassion. That would show me the way. Perhaps my tears would unlock something within so that love could be there—love that could hold everything, including the pain, the losses, the impermanence.

⸗ ∽∾ ⸗

Years earlier, there had been gifts that would assist Hob and me on this journey. I would recognize each one as it came, feeling grateful for the inspiration it offered us.

I remembered the day when our weekly meditation group had gathered at our friend Mary's house. It was the first meeting after a summer break. A brilliant warm September day, we had decided to meet outside. Mary, who was living with cancer, sat in a garden chair, her frail figure framed by morning glory vines abundant with blooms. Her vivid blue eyes were the same color as the morning glories. Physical diminishment somehow allowed her spirit to shine forth ever more radiantly.

Mary was a gifted artist. In one compelling series of paintings she explored the dance of life and death. Interwoven through blazing white bones were images of creepers, flowers, butterflies, birds, and children. She painted intricate realms of beings—animal, human, reptile, imaginary—some were underworlds, others were heavenly realms. Her images settled into one's psyche and took up residence there, ready to startle the viewer out of unexplored attitudes toward death. In Mary's vision, life and death existed in a seamless web. Like a warrior of the inner realms, she plunged into death's great mystery and invited us to accompany her.

For me, she was an inspiring elder, the embodiment of quiet wisdom. She and her husband, David, had long been the focal point of a lively community of people of all ages and walks of life, especially spiritual seekers. When Mary reached the later phases of her illness, a group of maybe ten to fifteen of their friends, including Hob and me, would gather around her bed every evening for meditation, a ritual that continued until the day she died. It was a memorable time, an example of how to open to death and invite others to participate in life's greatest passage.

On the morning of our gathering, Mary was holding a letter in her lap. She unfolded the blue pages with slow, careful movements.

"It's from an old friend," she explained. "She hasn't been in touch for a while and has written a long, thoughtful letter about dealing with physical limitations. There's a section I want to read which includes a reflection from Father Teilhard de Chardin, the philosopher and theologian. Here's how she paraphrases his words about growing older: 'In my younger years, I thanked God for my expanding, growing life; but now, in my later years, when I find my physical powers growing less, I thank God also for what I call the grace of diminishment.'"

At the end of our meeting, I copied those words and put them into a file entitled "Wisdom and Aging." That file would grow over the years, but perhaps the dearest treasure in it was those four words—"the grace of diminishment." When Hob was having a difficult time, I sometimes reopened Mary's gift and repeated those words to him. They were a reframing, an inspiration. Could we continue to live with the wisdom they invited?

—∞— ⟨∞⟩ —∞—

Drifting. That was a good word. Hob's energetic moorings to the world around were coming loose. The threads of connection were thinning, breaking. I was hauled reluctantly into looking at the reality of things with awakened eyes.

I searched for order in the midst of his confusion. I looked for something beyond what appeared to be wrong with him and pondered the hidden dimensions of our relationship. That was when I saw the image of a beautiful, complex weaving of filaments—psychic filaments like threads of multicolored light—that connect us to each other, especially to those we are in close relationship with. Like an intricate spider's web dancing in the wind, the filaments are resilient, dynamic, and flexible. As I visualized it then, and now, the threads of connection are most delicate in the heart area and most firmly connected in the diaphragm. They are especially strong there, where we stand most wedded over time; where the breath rises when it is deep and full. Breath. Life. Connection. That includes all the complicated, subtle karmas that we come together to work through in this life. It must be an intricate story that spans lifetimes.

When I saw Hob drifting, I felt the shock viscerally, in my gut. I could almost feel the psychic filaments of connection dissolving. The feelings of dissolution were sometimes gentle, sometimes ruthless. I learned to listen to the language of my gut, for that was where I often received the strongest messages. It spoke many languages: distress and tenderness, grief and protectiveness, fear and compassion.

Yet Hob's spiritedness still flashed forth. He played with words and sounds and associations like a child let loose in the great toy store of word games. It was alternately delightful and annoying for me. He would sometimes derail me in the middle of a conversation. As with so much else, I had to let go, be flexible, and honor that this playing was also the one continuous thread that he could hold on to as everything else slowly unraveled. What would happen when it was gone? (I caught it again: another useless, imponderable thought of the future.)

I wrote in my journal during this time: "How do I see this in terms of spiritual practice? Once again and forever—the great law of impermanence. I must try to live lightly and realize that the only refuge is calm, steady awareness. I must have faith in the inherent trustworthiness of the universe, no matter what happens. Why should anything be different from how it is now? It is just coming to us in this form."

How amazing! Another wake-up call. I was being shown in a new way how unconsciously we construct realities around the ones we love. We freeze everyone into a complex of fixed concepts about "who they are," or at least who we think they are. We assume familiar, predictable patterns of behavior. We spin a world of concepts, expectations, and assumptions, and then live relating to the world of our own creation more than to the reality of the person as he or she is in this moment. When a piece of carefully constructed reality falls away, we're caught unawares. We're left momentarily empty. "Where is he?" "What's going on here?"

I worried about how Hob's illness would unfold and how I

could handle everything. Then I'd catch myself and write bits of wisdom in my journal for inspiration. On the subject of worrying, I'd once heard the Dalai Lama say in one of his talks, "There's no benefit to worrying whatsoever." A simple enough statement, but as so often happens, we tend to pick up and remember the messages we'll need at some given time in our lives. Later I would read a similar message by Shantideva, the ninth-century philosopher, in his classic book, *A Guide to the Bodhisattva's Way of Life.*[2]

If you can solve your problem, then what is the need of worrying?

If you can't solve your problem, then what is the use of worrying?

He made it sound so simple. Worrying or not worrying, none of us in the family were finding this to be simple.

I noticed, for example, how our son Ethan responded to Hob's situation. I would see him looking intently at his father as if trying to take in something he couldn't see, maybe something Hob had said that didn't quite add up or that left broken threads of communication. In a flash of expressions, Ethan looked dismayed, let down, slightly impatient. All so understandable.

While accepting the range of feelings evoked, I needed to look beyond my limited vision of things. What mattered was the love that connected us, the love that was greater than what the mind did with all its creations. I kept reminding Hob and myself that love was the only thread that would hold, no matter what happened.

When I felt myself clinging intensely, I'd write mantras in my journal to inspire myself:

"Accept and let go . . . ," I wrote. "Breathe into your heart. . . . Let your heart be broken open with love. . . . We are being held. . . . The center will hold. . . . The center will hold because the center is the great heart. Especially when things are hard, take refuge in the luminous center, the heart of love."

Regardless of the journal entries and my other efforts to maintain normalcy amidst Hob's slow decline, I kept being taken by surprise. Periodically I was swamped under the weight of what needed to be done because he was no longer able to carry his weight in our lives: all those responsibilities of household chores, car problems, finances, our social life. On one particular afternoon, everywhere I looked things were screaming for attention: unsorted piles of stuff, errands undone, repairs needed, garden unweeded, a ripped screen. Even being outside in the garden failed to bring its usual delight. I felt a wave of outrage, totally out of proportion to the reality of the situation. How come the viburnum was obstructing the path so you had to duck to get by? How come the pansies had dried out—again—because no one had watered them? How could the rambling roses be spilling into our neighbor's driveway—again? Every uncompleted task rose up like a judgment against me, demanding an instant response.

By the end of the afternoon I felt weepy. Still I drove myself on—a mindless, desperate attempt to stay the flood. Finally, angry and exhausted, I sat down in a garden chair next to where Hob was reading and announced, "I think I just have to cry."

And I fell apart. Feelings of overwhelm poured forth. He drew closer, took my hands, listened, and tried to help. I felt completely desolate, and we were only in the early stages of things. Where had my resilience gone? Not a shred of awareness left. No remembrance of the breath or what might have been right action, according to Buddhist teachings, in situations like this one. What would that have been anyway? Right action would have been to stop. Sit down. Breathe. Go for a walk. Anything but the heedless course I had been locked into, like some crazed animal caught in a maze, running faster and faster with the hope of getting to the end of it.

I was beginning to recognize the patterns of what it was like to live with someone in early-stage dementia. I saw how mindless activity was the ultimate seduction. If I just kept going, doing something—anything!—I wouldn't have to feel all the losses.

Later, sitting around the table having iced tea with a friend who had come by for a visit, Hob began holding forth. In the presence of other people, he often seemed infused with new life. He began to make up comic scenarios about our family life that left us bent over with laughter.

When he couldn't find a word, he paused, concentrated through the silence, and muttered, "Let me out of this cage of words. *La cage des paroles*." His French was still intact.

With that, he threw back his head and laughed with his

whole body, his face flushed with happiness at his creation. He was fine for now. But me? That particular moment of crisis had passed, but I never knew when my feelings of brokenness might hit again.

⸙ ⟡ ⸙

That night I had a dream that arose directly out of the ashes of my afternoon meltdown. From the time I had first gone into therapy in my mid-twenties, I had developed a steady trust in the way dreams reveal the deeper levels of one's life and the issues that are asking for attention. I went through cycles of paying more or less attention to dreams, sometimes keeping dream journals for months at a time. Now in the most challenging time of my life, dreams became like signposts along the way. They were vivid, an invitation to attend to the gifts of the inner life, a source of guidance and wisdom.

I am on a beach with another woman, where we are on an expedition in search of something. Like archaeologists, we are digging in the sand. We know that something valuable is buried there. We dig up several large statues of horses. The first one is too small and I decide not to keep it. Then another appears. It's not clear whether it has been washed up on the beach or if it is the yield of my digging. But it is large and powerful, a statuesque horse of magnificent proportions. I comment to my woman friend about the famous dig in China where archaeologists discovered a stunning array of life-sized figures from the distant past, buried carefully to preserve them. This horse is like that, except for one startling,

56

troubling difference. Its nose and mouth are missing, the section from the round of its cheek forward. It is broken at a very strategic place. Should I keep it? It is broken. Flawed. I hesitate, wanting to leave it, to search further. But the woman, who is older and wiser than I, says, "No. No. Keep it. Look how magnificent it is, like the Venus de Milo or one of those glorious Greek statues raised from beneath the sea. The brokenness is part of what it is."

How do we accept our brokenness? That was a question I lived with now. Certainly there were long periods during which Hob's situation and my handling of it were in balance, and where life proceeded in many of its old, familiar ways. Yet at the same time, there were shocks that tipped the balance this way and that: his losses and confusion, my overwhelm and grief. I knew intellectually that brokenness opens us to compassion both for ourselves and for all who suffer, that it leads us out of isolation to feel our connection with all beings. Yet I was still fighting against a constellation of feelings that periodically arose: fragmentation, inadequacy, failure.

Even with the perplexing image of the horse's head, I felt inspired by the dream. The older, wiser woman was a part of my psyche, and she had given a compelling message. In spite of its impaired head, the horse was magnificent. The power of the images in the dream dwarfed and transformed my personal, momentary drama. The treasures had come from the unconscious—from beneath the sea—a reminder of the inspiration and healing that can come through dreams. Our brokenness is not to be ignored or cast aside, but experienced deeply and then integrated into the wholeness of who we are. That horse was not only magnificent, it was powerful, ancient, and free. So are we.

—— ❧ ——

Early that spring, the third year since Hob's diagnosis, a surprise blizzard dropped heavy wet snow and the shrubs and trees in our area were damaged extensively. Shortly after I came in from freeing the shrubs from their burdens of snow, Hob appeared at the door of my study. I knew by now that when he came unexpectedly, he had one of those reports from the interior that we had talked about earlier. He had some update on how he was feeling, and he had to tell me about it immediately before it escaped into the fogs of forgetfulness.

"I'm discouraged," he said heavily. "Things don't seem to be the way they're supposed to be." He was looking at the maple tree outside our window. During the storm, a large branch, raw and mangled, had splintered away from the trunk.

"There's our coat of arms. Just write down 'damaged tree.'"

There was another important tree in our lives. Hob had bought a cow pasture in northern Vermont in the mid-fifties and built a house there, his refuge from New York City where he was teaching in those days. The place in Vermont, on a beautiful mountainside facing the higher mountains to the West, became a much-loved gathering place for our family and friends.

At the top of the hillside stood one old maple tree, a solitary sentinel, crowning the upper meadow with its presence. In the last few years, our old friend had begun to die. We watched sadly as each spring fewer branches leafed out. There was something noble and valiant about how that tree stood through one winter after another, still a strong profile against the sky, but ever more vulnerable to wind and weather. For the first time that summer, I wondered who would go first—Hob or the great maple?

FINDING YOUR INNER RESOURCES
Reflections

＊ In the early stages, faced with the unknowns of an unpredictable illness, most of us are still dealing with issues of acceptance. It's helpful to remember that whatever we resist, deplore, or condemn only creates more suffering. Sometimes when I felt besieged by the challenges of caretaking, I'd remind myself that even dementia was "in the natural order of things." Reflect on what helps to deepen acceptance for you.

＊ Given the nature of Alzheimer's, we increasingly live on the edge of the unknown: words gone, skills eroded, affect fading, and so on. The patient and the caregiver—perhaps in different ways—will be struck repeatedly by disbelief, shock, distress, overwhelm, and fear. Even the positive qualities we wish to cultivate may vanish amidst the struggles we are experiencing.

It helps to find something positive that you can remember in hard times, something enduring in your relationship. We tried to remember that love—ours as well as others'—was the thread that would hold us no matter what happened. Depending on your relationship to the person with Alzheimer's, you may prefer some other word like affection, fondness, loyalty, devotion, or compassion. These are the enduring states that can sustain us through anything.

* When your loved one's condition is variable and ultimately deteriorating, it helps to acknowledge— even embrace—the inevitability of change and loss. Constantly living with uncertainty can be unsettling and frightening, yet it is also an invitation for us to develop strength and equanimity.

* The words of Teilhard de Chardin are inspiring. In his late years, he could both appreciate the expansive energy of his youth and accept in old age "the grace of diminishment." There can be sadness and grief—even anger—in the diminishments caused by age and illness. Yet there can be hidden blessings: slowing down, simplifying one's life, discovering joy in small things—to name a few of the gifts of aging.

Suggestions

* Following from the previous reflection, can you find any blessings in your situation? Can you find even grace?

* It is human nature to close down and contract in the face of a serious illness. We may assume that friends will pull back and avoid us. This may be true occasionally, but most people want to respond when friends are in need. That's important to remember—especially for those who are hesitant to ask for help.

* An invaluable guideline for us was not to sink into isolation but to open into connection with family and friends. Do everything you can to keep this illness from isolating you. Break through your hesitance or inertia and keep reaching out. It will make the world of difference.

* What shared life experiences will remind you of your good times together? Retell these stories. Memories are treasures—golden threads that reconnect you to something positive and happy in your shared past. Later, when words are gone, you can tell these stories again and again, because feelings remain for the Alzheimer's patient even when the mind is seriously impaired.

* Are there songs, biblical quotations, or poems that are particularly loved? For us, poetry and music were sources of connection and joy until the end. It may be as little as one line from a song, as for us with the line, "All I want for you is forever to remember me as loving you." Such little things can become lifelines in the disappearing world of the patient. I came to think

61

of them as talismans that helped us along a difficult journey.

Seed Thoughts

May I remember the positive things that uplift us.

May I accept the surprises of this illness.

I can reach out for help at any time.

CHAPTER THREE

A DIFFERENT TRUTH

Hob and I were walking along barefoot in the warm sand accompanied by the rolling sound of ocean waves. Clusters of willets and sandpipers wove meandering patterns as they fed along the edge of the surf. They darted suddenly up the sloping beach to stay ahead of the foaming surf, then paused to thrust hungry bills into the damp sand. It was the third day of a vacation by the beach, and we were engaged in the easy conversation that unfolds when exploring a new place away from the demands of daily life.

"Someone said that a mile or so up the beach we'd come to the marshes where the bird watching is really good," Hob reported.

I was walking slowly, perusing the piles of shells gathered in mounds at the top of the tide line. Searching for shells was my favorite pastime whenever I got to a beach, especially this one, famous for its shelling.

"Maybe we can walk up there this afternoon," I responded, aware that the morning was almost gone. I knew the wisdom of keeping our days simple, because Hob tended to get overloaded by too much activity, one of the subtle signs of his illness.

He started to speak again. "Can fee ti loo . . ."

"What did you say?" I asked.

I stopped walking and turned toward him. He hesitated for a long heavy moment then spoke again.

"Cor be fuba haf . . ."

I listened intently, searching for clues, perplexed by what was going on. His words were there, then gone—from sense to nonsense in a moment. In the time it had taken us to walk four or five steps along this beautiful beach, a hidden event had occurred. Something had happened in his brain. Some circuit broken.

Suddenly I was alert and awake in every pore of my body. Instantly I became an archaeologist of sound, trying to decipher some meaning in the scattered syllables. As we continued to walk slowly along the beach, I focused on each step, each breath. An expectant silence shimmered between us.

I felt as if I'd been catapulted into another dimension of reality—jolted awake by the shock of his sudden confusion where words had unraveled into meaninglessness from one sentence to the next. Were his words going to come back, as they had when this happened the first time?

One day about a year before, we had overscheduled ourselves. He had gone to a long meeting in the morning. We had negotiated for and bought a new car in the afternoon, and then, as if that wasn't enough for one day, we attended the ballet that evening. By intermission it was clear that Hob was unsettled and exhausted. We skipped the second half of the performance and headed home. I sensed that he was struggling in some unfamiliar way; he was moving slowly, hesitating and stopping as he prepared for bed. He stood absentmindedly by the bed, fumbling with the buttons on his shirt. He started to say something, but his words fragmented into a stream of brokenness.

"Ish ke tobble frut . . ." He looked startled. Then he tried to speak again.

"Libble te cora vi . . ." He shook his head slightly, looking puzzled, stunned. He waited.

Then, as if gathering himself at some other level, he looked intently at me and said, "I'm clear."

There was a long pause. Now I was the one to be startled. Then he spoke again and repeated the statement with emphasis. "I'm clear," he said, his brow furrowed with concentration.

But his next effort to speak collapsed again into nonsensical syllables. At first I couldn't figure out what was going on, how he could be speechless one moment and able to tell me he was clear in the next.

Both of us floundered in this new realm of aborted communication. In an intuitive flash, I realized he was telling me that even if he couldn't respond intelligibly, he could still understand me.

"Let's not even try to talk," I'd replied. "It's okay. It's just a passing event. Let's get ready for bed."

That night, I figured he must have had a T.I.A., a transient ischemic attack, or some kind of occlusion in the brain, fairly common in elders, especially with Alzheimer's. The next morning his words were back. He was able to describe what he had been experiencing while his words were scrambled.

"As a survivor of my own process last night," he said, "I realized that I had a kind of double vision. Inside here, I'm thinking, 'I'm fine,' and I was able to tell you with those words, 'I'm clear.'"

But today? Questions streamed through my mind as we continued to walk along the beach. I waited. How could I not wonder if this was the end of his speech?

Silence between us. Only the sound of the surf and some gulls shrieking over a contested piece of garbage. Attentive as a mother watching her child, I followed every nuance of his movement. Did he know what was happening? Was he fearful? Or frustrated, suspended in some realm of disconnection?

Another memory flashed into mind of an episode from almost thirty years earlier. Hob had cut an article out of the Princeton Alumni magazine and carefully put it into his sundry file, the place where he kept special items. But first he had invited me to read the article, and afterward we'd had a long discussion about its implications.

The widow of a Princeton alumnus had written an article for the magazine. She began with a brief portrait of her husband's life: how he had been an all-American football hero, later decorated for valor in World War II. He returned from the war to become a family man and the CEO of a major company. Years later in his mid-sixties, he was diagnosed with Alzheimer's disease, and this was where the article became compelling. After several years of living with the disease, rather than tolerate more suffering for his family and himself, he decided to choose the time and manner of his own death. He and his wife had discussed all of this ahead of time. She had fully supported his choice. One night he left a note, walked to the beach, plunged into a stormy sea, and ended his life.

The article had deeply affected Hob. Even though taking one's life at any time is a controversial matter, in the face of his disease this man had made a courageous decision, one that appeared right to him. Hob clearly identified with the story and expressed his admiration for the man's decision.

"He chose the noble route," he said. "He made the choice to die the Roman way, the decision to end life on your own terms. I think it's more honorable and dignified to choose one's way of going rather than be reduced to mute idiocy or helpless dependency."

When Hob was diagnosed, this conversation was one of the first things I remembered—how we had talked about his fellow alumnus and the article by his widow which Hob had kept. Had he had some premonition? Or was it simply one more instance of his openness to the subject of death and his willingness to look squarely into the inevitable.

"Hobbie, let's go for a swim. I think that might be the best thing to do right now. No need for any words."

He looked past me and nodded. Hob loved the water and was a strong swimmer. I watched as he waded into the surf, waited for the right wave, then dove into the wall of water and began to swim strongly away from the beach, far beyond the breaking surf.

I continued to watch his long, graceful strokes, and yet became aware that I was absorbed with a more vivid image—the memory of that other man, years earlier, who had headed into the sea to end his life. I was left with an eerie feeling, like an echo. Abruptly, I took off and ran down the short expanse of beach into the surf. I felt propelled by a determination to wash away the discomfort of that man's choice.

Later that afternoon, Hob's words returned. We were sitting silently together on the beach outside our little cabin to watch the sunset. I realized gratefully that we'd negotiated another incident in this journey toward the unknown. Even though that helped to assuage my uneasy feelings about Hob's episodes of aphasia, after-images of the beach episode kept cycling into my mind: Hob struggling for words, blurting out nonsense syllables, something about him feeling broken.

As I sat with him, memories flashed forth, in stark contrast to the episode of loss on the beach. In my mind's eye, like images on a filmstrip, I glimpsed Hob in the fullness of who he was before illness took hold.

One evening, I remembered, he was standing in the front of a church, a member of the Noonday Singers who were in the middle of another concert, singing songs of hope and struggle from the peace and social justice movement. Hob stepped forward from the group to introduce one of his favorite songs, entitled "Tumamena," a South African freedom song.

"These were the songs that helped the South Africans survive the oppression of apartheid," he explained to the audience.

"Many of you have probably heard of Robben Island, the infamous prison where Nelson Mandela was imprisoned for twenty-eight years. Well, in those prisons, when one of the prisoners was being marched through the hallway toward his execution, his fellow prisoners would lean through the bars of their cells and start singing. This was one of their songs. It's called "Tumamena," hauntingly beautiful, a kind of prayer. Imagine them singing this song as the condemned prisoner disappeared through the door to his death."

The Noonday Singers broke into song—one verse in South African, the next in English. "Lead me Jesus, lead me Lord. Hold me Jesus, hold me Lord." Hob was singing so passionately, he seemed to be in that prison, a prisoner himself, singing his heart out, certain that freedom could triumph over everything.

Hob loved to sing and our family life was filled with music. He had a Martin guitar which he took along wherever he went so he could practice a Bach suite, sing sixties folk songs, or serenade Ethan and Laura to sleep with lullabies. Guitar or no guitar, he'd often break into song at unexpected moments, parodying a chorus from Gilbert and Sullivan, playing with the words of "Puff the Magic Dragon," or dropping his voice to the bottom of his range, obviously enjoying the resonance and depth of his bass voice.

On the other hand, ever the musical taskmaster, he had his impatient, intolerant side. On long car trips when we had family marathons of singing rounds, if we failed to get our part right in "A Sad and Weary Wanderer," a tricky Mozart round, he would jump on us mercilessly and our singing would collapse into grumbles and family insurrection. End of rounds.

Then another fleeting image, this time of Hob with our daughter, Laura, both of them cast members in the Christmas Revels, an annual performance to celebrate the winter solstice, a feast of pageantry, dance, and song. The curtain had risen for the second act on a ballroom scene set in Victorian times.

Hob was dressed in white tie and tails. Laura, although only thirteen, looked elegant in a full-length, long-sleeved dress of golden silk with lace at the neck. Her long brown hair was pulled up into a bun, and she was wearing white gloves. When the strains of the waltz began, Hob moved toward Laura in an invitation to the dance. They spun across the stage with the other dancers, father and daughter delighting in the thrill of performance and in dancing with one another—a cameo moment for both of them, now a poignant memory for me.

That's how it was for us as family members: we lived with Hob's slow decline; it was a dance of past and present, the memories and losses all interwoven, tugging us back and forth between realities.

At the time of Hob's diagnosis, he was seventy-two and I was fifty-eight. In one way, the timing was fortuitous. I had recently resigned from a full-time job teaching at the Mind/Body Clinic at a major Boston hospital, a job that I had loved. In one of the first programs of its kind in the country, we had pioneered how to bring meditation, yoga, and cognitive therapy into a medical setting. We taught stress management to a wide array of outpatient clinics and trained health professionals through Harvard Medical School.

Exciting as it had been to be on the cutting edge in the field of Behavioral Medicine, as I moved into my late fifties, I decided to leave a high-pressure job for a more balanced life. I began to experiment with how to move into a new phase, where, having left an institutional setting, I needed to create my own structures. I continued to teach meditation and do part-time counseling, and began to write. Increasingly, my life expanded to include the joyful dimension of becoming a grandparent, more time for friendship, being with the dying, attending births, visiting with elders—the rich mix of becoming an elder myself.

Naturally Hob's situation added another dimension to my life. It created a whole new ever-changing set of challenges. Although he was still relatively independent, I was aware of my deep need for space and time alone. Even though we now had the part-time help of Diane, a natural caregiver with lightness of spirit and sense of humor, I experienced the subtleties of caregiving as wearying.

Caregiving—the new dimension—an immersion that

happened so gradually that I needed to remind myself periodically to step back and appreciate how much energy it was taking. It was like falling into a fast-flowing river; I was so busy trying to negotiate the swirling, rapid currents, I would forget the magnitude of what we were dealing with. Much of it was invisible. The psychic toll was the heaviest. I needed to be aware—immensely aware—all the time. I lived on the edge of the moment, always awaiting the next gap.

"What's her name, that woman who . . . " or "You know the word I want . . ." or "Where were we when . . . ?" I lived relating almost more to the gaps than to the person.

It is difficult to describe what it was like to live in relationship to Hob's disintegrating mind. When I was conscious about it and called on the resources of my Buddhist practice, it was like sitting on my meditation cushion: my field of awareness was light and alert, open to whatever might arise. More than ever, this approach began to permeate my life with Hob. The moment I walked into his presence, I shifted into a heightened awareness.

This practice was charged with intensity because it wasn't my own repetitive, well-worn mental patterns emerging, but his unpredictable ones. Sometimes they were freighted with feeling. There was urgency or impatience, anxiety or fear. He rarely spoke about his fear, but when he did, I could feel the force of it, like molten lava beneath the surface. My job was not just to "fill in the gaps"; it was being finely attuned to his world. I needed to be open to receive and respond to unanticipated depth charges from his psyche. I never knew what was coming. Sometimes it was something funny and we would break into laughter. There was the moment he asked, "What's the name of that disease I have? Horse blinders?"

No mistaking what he meant or the humorous way he referred to it: "horse blinders," a playful rhyme to match "Alzheimer's." Other times what he said was tinged with frustration or alarm, as when he asked, "Can you come back from this strange land from which most don't return because the words are gone?"

I lived in constant challenge. I needed to patrol the borders of my personal boundaries so I didn't lose myself in being his indispensable "other." Yet, simultaneously, I had to remain receptive and accepting of those intrusions of his psychic need. I was humbled, sometimes daunted, by the enormity of all of it. But I knew we'd make it, whatever "it" turned out to be.

Anyone who by-stands a partner with Alzheimer's lives in several worlds at once. There was Hob's life and the complexities of the disease. There was my life apart from his. And then there was our world together, which interfaced with our family and friends—a distinctly different world from before, for it had now been a couple of years since his diagnosis. I became his intermediary, helping him with plans and tasks, negotiating with health professionals, serving as interpreter between his world and our friends. Sometimes I needed to prepare them, explaining the latest changes. Or I might serve as midwife to conversation, the finder of names and words and meanings.

All this was like a delicate dance. Increasingly, I felt the challenge of this role: wanting to honor his independence, protect his dignity, and keep our lives as so-called normal as possible. All the while, the ground was shifting under him and therefore under me as well.

As for me, I was grateful when someone acknowledged the complexity and challenge of it all. It's common knowledge that caring for someone with any illness can be an isolating experience. I had several friends who called regularly to check in, see how we were doing, and send love. One of them was Margot. She was one of my mother's oldest friends, and a life-long spiritual seeker. That fall, about two years after the diagnosis, she suggested that both Hob and I meet someone with whom she had been working.

Only visiting for a couple of weeks, John was a Taoist healer, she explained. He had been seriously wounded in Vietnam and had lingered at the edge of death, his head and body peppered with shrapnel. He survived that critical time and then spent many years trying to regain his health, working with healers here and in Asia. John himself developed the gift of healing and was encouraged by his teachers to serve others. The prospect of seeing him seemed like divine intercession to me; it came in the midst of a week of feeling burdened, exhausted.

The sessions with John were held in Margot's meditation room, a quiet, welcoming space with a low altar against the wall, above which hung a colorful Tibetan *thankha*, a scroll that depicts symbolic scenes from Tibetan cosmology. There were a couple of photographs of Margot's teachers, a vase of yellow tulips, and a candle whose flickering light reflected off the statue of the Buddha that was the centerpiece of the altar.

Hob had his session first. When he came out of the room, I sensed that he was deeply indrawn, surrounded by quiet. His face was relaxed and soft, his expression open and childlike. He looked at me as if from a distance and said, "That was really good. But I think I'll rest now and stay quiet. You go ahead in. John's waiting for you."

My session began with some preliminary conversation, as John inquired about what was going on in my life. After I made myself comfortable on the couch, John simply sat with me. Most of the time he sat quietly in meditation, "tuning in" and "clearing through" as he had described it, allowing and encouraging a healing process that was mysterious and unnamable. I found myself in a very deep state, mind totally still, body deeply relaxed, suspended in a timeless, loving place.

Elusive as it is to measure energy work, he had helped me to shift into a more balanced, serene state. Afterward I felt lighter, unburdened, and very spacious, especially around the heart area, as if knots of tension, worry, and anxiety had unraveled and dissolved. That experience of a healing spaciousness stayed with me for days afterward, leaving me grateful that it had helped me reconnect with my own sources of healing.

We arranged a second session for Hob on the following day. Afterward, once again, Hob wanted to rest. John pulled me aside to talk. This was not a breach of confidentiality, he explained, but hopefully he might be of help.

"I wanted to let you know how struck I have been while sitting with Hob by the tremendous intensity of his feelings. As you know our sessions are mostly silent, but you don't need any words to feel in the silence how much he is like a nuclear reactor. That's the intensity that this process of mental loss is creating in him."

He paused. "And that's also what you're living with all the time. I'm sure you know it, but sometimes it's helpful to have a reality check from others."

How well I knew! I had my own images for Hob's intensity; sometimes I felt what seemed like a molten lava flow of feelings beneath the surface. I wondered if it would help him to talk with a therapist with a specialty in dementia, or whether he was beyond that process. So far he'd turned to a few trusted friends, not therapists, to deal with his illness. And he had relied on his meditation practice. Left to himself he would seldom remember to meditate, but the two of us sat together regularly. He told me that in some ways meditation was more effortless now than before. Interesting. So many dimensions of inner experience to learn about. Yes, there was grace even in the midst of this disease.

⁘ ⚬⚬ ⁘

One crisp, cold morning in early winter, late fallen oak leaves danced across the terrace on a high wind. Just as I was getting ready to leave for a morning meeting, the telephone rang. Let me leave that call for the answering machine, I thought, but at the last moment something prompted me to pick up the phone.

At the other end of the line, Hob announced, "My car's been towed. I don't know how it happened. I didn't see any signs not to park there. I'm at the White Hen Pantry. Can you come and get me?"

The strain in his voice betrayed the distress he was in. Here again was the unexpected moment, the need for an abrupt about-face at the start of a morning that didn't include this agenda item. The hassle of retrieving the car would make me very late for my meeting, an event I was partially responsible for having set up.

As I hung up the phone, I could feel the pounding of my heart, the surge of heat in my belly. It had already been a rocky morning because of his missing date-book and the frantic scurrying around as we both searched for it. I began invoking patience in an effort to fight off the mounting anger, but the inner battle was already in full force.

When I reached the store from where he had called, I saw him standing behind the glass doors—a solitary figure—waiting, forlorn, looking out for my arrival. In the sea of early morning traffic, I could stop for only a moment. I waved brightly and blew the horn. He didn't move. He continued to stand there looking blankly out into the street. Then, inexplicably, he turned away.

It was a heartbreaking moment. As I drove around the building to park, I felt driven into desolation by that glimpse of him through the door. What was wrong? Had he not seen me? Not recognized the car? When I walked into the store and asked him what had happened, he merely said, "Well, I guess I didn't see you. Sorry."

Another disconnection, another sign. Even though I could recognize this little melodrama for what it was, I couldn't restrain my rage over what had happened. In some slender place of knowing, I realized that the build-up of frustration to anger was a cumulative process, extended over days and weeks and months. I could only stand by and watch the insidious deterioration of his mind. Everything in me wanted to scream and shake him and say, "Stop! Wake up! You don't have to be this way!"

But a terrible silence greeted that thought. Was my disbelief not one of the persistent illusions of this journey? Some part of me kept thinking he was pretending—and I knew the absurdity of that.

When I finally dropped him off at the towing company and drove away toward my meeting, I collapsed into fury. No matter that I was totally aware of what was happening. This time, after all the previous times of letting frustration go, I had to let the full force of my feelings break free. Images of Kali, the dark goddess of the Hindu pantheon, arose out of nowhere. She was wildly dancing, she who symbolizes the destruction and death that leads to transformation. I bellowed and roared.

I struggled to release the sound from deep in my belly where the rage resided. At first, nothing seemed to expiate the enormity of the feelings. I understood then how people had terrible accidents spawned from rage and, horrified, realized that I, too, could have done something violent, could have crashed the car, or worse. I was in the clutches of a primal force. I had to face it, experience it, and finally accept that this, too, was part of me.

Mysteriously, the roaring began to transform into a wild chant, a chant to Kali, which I'd heard in India years before. At first it seemed like weak, ineffectual medicine, but after a number of rounds of the chant, its power began to work; the fire of anger gradually subsided into pure energy charging through my body, and finally to a deep calm. It was amazing even to me that all this had happened in a matter of a few minutes while I continued driving to my meeting. Somehow, out of the pressure of the situation, a way through had come to me. Sound—any kind of sound—was a great way to expiate frustration and anger.

"So, what do you do with your anger?" an older friend whose spouse also had Alzheimer's had once asked me. I told him how often it took me by surprise, that in truth I was shocked because by nature I wasn't a person who angered easily. On the contrary. Except for the inevitable strains of child rearing and the occasional cross-rips that occur in any marital relationship, I had always lived with a fairly high degree of equanimity. I simply was not, by nature, an angry person.

How startling then, I confessed to him, to discover that anger was something I now needed to accept and work with.

Quite simply, the strains of helping Hob with his disease kept stretching me to the breaking point. My frustration and anger also concealed the grief that lay at deeper levels. But there was hardly room for grief. The call was always to move on to the next challenge, to remain steady and calm, because that was what he needed.

Early on, I told my friend, I had realized that there was no one to blame for the situations that ignited my frustration. I could no longer reason through some tangled place of relationship with Hob because he hadn't meant to create the tangle in the first place. There was no ill intention. No malice. As the *I Ching*, the Chinese book of changes, says, "No blame."

No blame. Even though I often called upon that phrase to calm my anger, it didn't change the reality I lived with. Occasionally, a surge of frustration or anger flipped me back to some earlier scene in our relationship, some painful moment that had festered, sometimes for years, beneath the surface of things, until a trigger reawakened it.

When Ethan and Laura were eight and five, I came down with pneumonia, not sick enough to be hospitalized but I was bedridden for days—weak, discouraged, and heavy-hearted. Being really sick is a nightmare for mothers of young children. Naturally, the last thing on my mind was an unfinished project that stood neglected on our front stoop.

The previous summer our family had hiked to the summit of Mt. Abraham across the valley from our Vermont house. As we picnicked on a large rock outcropping at the top of the mountain,

I noticed the abundance of dwarfed trees, hemlocks that looked like bonsai in the wild. They were naturally stunted and shaped by the harsh mountain winters. Intrigued by a friend's bonsai garden, I carefully dug up one of the hemlocks and carried the little tree down the mountain, planted it temporarily in an old foil pan, then took it back to Cambridge where I intended to find a suitable pot into which to transplant it.

I never quite got around to replanting that little tree. One January day as I lay abed with pneumonia, feeling wretched at the nadir of the illness, Hob appeared in the doorway of our bedroom holding the muddy pan with my forlorn would-be bonsai.

"Why haven't you planted this yet?" he asked. "It's been sitting on the front steps for altogether too long."

His voice was judgmental and accusatory, as cold as the icicles that clung to its branches. Stunned to silence, I turned away and began to weep silently.

It was one of those excruciating moments in our relationship when both of us, feeling wounded for different reasons, collided in midstream. I couldn't believe he'd hit me with something so inconsequential when I was struggling for breath, down and out. I already felt vulnerable, too exhausted to express the hurt and anger that would fester later on.

We had several spicy postmortems about that moment. How could someone with Hob's sensitivity have been so totally out of touch with what I needed at that time? Like everyone, he had his dark, unconscious side from which he sometimes lashed out, hurting before he realized the impact of his words. Eventually I realized how symbolic the whole scene had been. First of all, he found it unbearable that I was so sick. Out of worry and fear of abandonment he had struck out like a mindless, wounded child; it was some old pattern in him triggered by my frailty. Perhaps he'd been trying to get me to respond in my usual upbeat way. And perhaps because of his painful childhood with years of humiliation from being physically stunted, he identified with that little tree as it sat stunted and neglected on the front step, much as he himself had felt as a bereft child. What seemingly minuscule encounters can stir the hottest feelings!

Now, in the midst of his illness, surprised by how caretaking amplified my feelings, I realized how much any irritation on my part upset Hob. That helped me to find new ways to deal with my irritation. With a rush of compassion, I realized that his defenses were gone. He had lost what I called his "psychic shield," the mechanisms that protect us from the full impact of all kinds of stimuli. Now he was open and vulnerable, permeable like some soft creature without its shell. Sadly, with his unbearable sensitivity, he could hardly tolerate the exuberant energy of our two grandsons. Too much stimulus of any kind sent him into a downward spiral of recoil and confusion. I watched for signs of sensory overload. I walked the psychological tightrope between keeping his life stimulating and keeping it simple.

As my irritation escalated, I watched as it occasionally erupted into anger over meaningless details, like the morning when the English muffins weren't ready in time for the eggs and then I ended up burning them anyway. First I felt the anger rising, then, almost immediately, a moment of recognition: my flare of anger struck me as so disproportionate, I had to figure out what triggered it.

In a flash of insight, I recognized that any disease involves the loss of control over things as they have been—the body's health, the mind's clarity, one's daily life. Day by day, our life together was dying. The burned English muffins revealed how easily my wish for everything to go along smoothly could capsize in a moment. And surely feelings of helplessness and grief compounded the situation and threw it out of all proportion.

I gradually learned coping mechanisms that worked for me: finding time to be alone, taking a walk, working out vigorously, or talking with friends. Finally, there was roaring. Several times, I walked out of the house with such a build-up of intensity that my ultimate refuge was the car. There I could release all my volcanic feelings by roaring—repetitive roaring, the roars of a caged wild animal. I roared until the rage was spent and copious tears spilled over.

Then there was the other extreme—a totally different response to the same triggers. As I gained insight into the dynamics of my anger, whenever I felt that first flash, I would move in a counterintuitive direction. I could feel the moment of inner shift. There was a split-second pause, with its delicate balance point. I would sink deep into the next breath and choose to expand instead of contract. Choose softness instead of hardness. I would move toward Hob, sometimes in silence, other times saying, "I need a hug."

With our physical closeness, the anger invariably dissolved. Touch was always the most comforting, powerful response for us both. Subtle and invisible, these shifts felt like little triumphs. Every time, they amazed me. Like practicing anything new, the more I did it, the easier it became. There were more and more moments of grace, and ultimately I learned the most heartening way to deal with anger.

About three years after Hob's diagnosis, I remembered a meditation retreat where I had walked into an interview with one of the teachers. I sat down in a chair opposite him, took a deep breath, and declared that I needed to talk about anger and death. That's called leading with the big issues! The teacher knew both of us well, and I appreciated the sensitivity and depth of his response.

"This situation with Hob is teaching you how to die," he responded quietly in answer to my statement.

"Everything's falling apart. You need to feel it, all of it—your frustration, your anger, your grief, whatever—and experience your full humanness. Accept that the old securities are collapsing. It's all going, and it's showing you the process of death. This is the biggest thing you've ever done, so you need to be easier on yourself!"

Showing me the process of death. Those were illuminating words. Of course I knew that Hob was in the final chapter of his life, but I hadn't focused on how much I was living in a parallel process. Together we were learning about loss and acceptance, letting go and death. This was hard, but these were the gifts.

Writing became one of my places of refuge. Refuge—that evocative word from the Buddhist tradition that invites us to turn to what is eternal for inspiration and support. Refuge suggests safety; a time or place set apart from ordinary life for silence and solitude; for meditation, quiet, and a return to the center of being.

Amidst the demands of living with someone who had brain disease, meditation was, naturally, a refuge. Yet the concept of refuge in Buddhism also reminds us that, even in solitude, we remain at subtle levels connected to others. For if we think about it deeply, the mere thought of another creates an experience of connection. That sense of connectedness is also a form of refuge. Buddhist teachings describe three places of refuge for the practitioner, which are known as the three jewels. First, we take refuge in the wise ones. For Hob and me, given years of practicing in this tradition, it was the Buddha, the one who dedicated himself to discovering the causes of suffering and how to find freedom from that suffering; and who, after his enlightenment, spent fifty years of his life teaching how that was possible. For other traditions, the same principle applies; seekers turn for inspiration to Jesus, Mother Mary, Mohammed, the goddess, or other embodiments of wisdom and compassion.

The second refuge is the dharma, the Sanskrit word for the truth, or the way to the truth. Again, whatever the spiritual tradition, the principles of devotion and observance of the practices show us the way to meet the challenges of life, and so they are likened to a vehicle that carries us across the symbolic oceans, mountains, and deserts of human existence.

Finally, we take refuge in the *sangha*, or community. This can mean everyone from our fellow seekers to the wise ones of all times—buddhas, bodhisattvas, Jesus, the prophets, the great rabbis—any being who is a source of inspiration for us.

At a meditation retreat, still early in Hob's illness, I recalled the simple invitation of one of my dharma teachers.

"Be gentle with yourself, Olivia, be gentle. And know what your refuges are."

Her compassionate words allowed me to ease into what felt like bottomless sadness. Even though still near the beginning of this journey, already I was struggling with the strains of care-giving. I needed every possible refuge, and the idea took on new levels of meaning. By then I realized that it included the support of friendship, time alone in nature, or occasionally the loving care of massage therapy. "Know what your refuges are" become important words for anyone by-standing a spouse or family member with serious illness.

In addition to the refuges, there were the philosophical perspectives that inspired and sustained me. These were like touchstones for both Hob and me. Obviously, the journey with Alzheimer's was what we had been called to in the last chapter of his life. In connection with this came two realizations that inspired both of us. These were crucial to finding meaning in what life had handed us.

First and most important, I reminded myself that we must have agreed, on the soul level, to go through this experience together. Such a statement demands explanation. As I see it, our lives have many levels. There are the obvious ones like family, relationships, work, interests, and activities. There is our life story, with its joys and sorrows, its triumphs and failures, its loves and losses. There is the spiritual level, how each of us relates to the great mystery of life: the miracle of the human body, the wonders of nature, and the inexplicable—birth and death, visions and dreams, synchronicities and miracles. I would call this the soul level, this particular life we incarnate into, with its particularities and patterns.

I believe that nothing is random in our lives. If one holds, even remotely, the possibility that our lives unfold in some innate order, then we are here to learn, work through, and, hopefully, transform the difficulties that come our way.

Hob once alluded to this when he was talking about his attitude toward the disease.

"I accept whatever is ordained for it to be," he had said.

And another time, after some difficult episode, he reassured me and articulated his feelings about the disease with this thoughtful observation:

"It's not to be worried about," he said. "It's a different truth."

This was a profound statement. I would remember his words; they pointed to something deeper than the rational mind's attempts to understand the subtler dimensions of this illness. This was a call to investigate deeply as we went along, not to assume that Alzheimer's would proceed in predestined ways, not to allow the usual reactivity and fear to distort the experience, while also knowing that fear of the unknown—particularly of losing the mind—is one of the deepest human fears.

I saw his illness as in the natural order of things. It felt like a shared destiny, a karmic fulfillment. I knew I would have to keep reframing our experience in that context, that this would be one of the keys to our passage through whatever lay ahead. At the deepest level, what mattered most was our commitment to live this journey as consciously and lovingly as possible. That was our shared task.

The second realization was that this was our practice. When I remembered that, the challenges of the days seemed natural, even easy. Sometimes there were moments when I'd feel exhilarated by the challenges of deciphering his disconnected phrases. I felt like I was an archaeologist of the mind, digging for meaning. I dusted off the phrases, hoping to discover the treasures hidden beneath the surface of garbled speech. When I got it, he would be delighted. So was I! Such were the small pleasures of this journey.

And was it ever important to appreciate those small pleasures! For no sooner had we had settled into a phase where life seemed to be sailing along on a more even keel, than the next unexpected episode would blow us both over. It was inevitable, but that doesn't mean either of us was ever ready for it. Hob had described how living with Alzheimer's felt like living with "a different truth." His words came back to me from time to time. But how could we possibly sustain the detached perspective they suggested?

DEALING WITH FEELINGS
Reflections

∗ With Alzheimer's, as with any serious illness, we discover that we are powerless in the face of an inexorable and uncontrollable process. Our powerlessness is a painful realization, and each of us will find our own ways of dealing with it. We might turn to our faith, join a support group, talk with friends, throw ourselves into some new activity, or surrender to its inevitability. The first step is to recognize it.

∗ Dealing with the spectrum of feelings that both patient and caregiver will experience can be daunting. For either of you, the smallest incident can trigger intense emotions: anger, grief, fear, or despair. As you think about the person with dementia, can you "walk in her shoes" and imagine what these losses are like for her, how distressing it must be to be unable to find words, much less handle increasingly perplexing situations. Whenever we can open with compassion toward ourselves and others, it will provide some comfort, because the heart softens. Instead of separation, whether from our own heart or the other person, we feel connection.

* It's worth repeating that the ravages of illness spark powerful feelings in everyone, perhaps more intense— even more fearfully so—than ever before. We need to experience our humanness, including all the so-called dark emotions like anger and fear, because they are natural given the situation. It's natural to think you're losing it at times. You may need to allow strong feelings to run their course, yet be vigilant about not taking them out on others.

* The caregiver, family, and friends are living in a parallel process to the patient. Together you are experiencing continual changes, innumerable losses, and mortality issues, as well as all the strong feelings they evoke. These are some of the subtleties of caregiving, and they are often invisible to others. Naturally, both patient and caregiver experience loneliness and despair. That's why reaching out for companionship and help is so important.

Suggestions

* When you feel as if you are on an emotional roller coaster, remember that you can be clear about your feelings in one instance but feel confused or lost in another. For example, helplessness may underlie anger; exhaustion can trigger frustration; grief can

spawn hopelessness; fatigue may hide grief, and so on, in infinite combinations. We forget the cumulative impact of small incidences on us as caregivers.

* See if you can identify the coping mechanisms that help you when intense emotions arise. For me grieving was usually a solitary process, though sometimes eased by journaling or being with a family member or friend. In the case of anger, vigorous exercise or a walk were especially helpful. I also sometimes turned to an art journal where I did symbolic drawings with oil pastels to express my feelings. When I felt overwhelmed, I went off in the car and roared. Do whatever you can to channel your feelings into constructive avenues.

* Similarly, know what your refuges are. At one time, I posted a list in a prominent place because I couldn't remember my inner resources in the heat of the moment. Examples: put on music, do expressive art, write, work in the garden, exercise, do something— anything!—that's different and fun.

* In instances when I felt frustrated or angry, it was a revelation when I discovered an effective, counter-intuitive response. As I took several deep breaths, the intensity of my feelings would start to soften, and I would reach out for physical contact or ask for a hug. It felt like changing course in midstream: instead of the impending emotional collision, I experienced a

shift in my feelings and, with it, a sense of release and tenderness. Awareness allows for choice, and this is the practice of choosing love instead of conflict.

* It is an agonizing process to watch how Alzheimer's destroys the mind. It is hard to find any meaning in what appears to be a cruel and meaningless process. Nevertheless, we can shift our perspectives or have new insights about even the most difficult circumstances. Reflect on these questions:

What am I being called to by this situation?

What is this illness demanding of me, and how can I respond most caringly to our circumstances, however hard they may be?

What qualities am I being asked to develop?

Seed Thoughts

May I cultivate compassion toward myself and others.

I trust my ability to handle whatever comes up.

May I find new ways of handling my negative emotions.

CHAPTER FOUR

GET YOUR DYIN' DONE EARLY

Back in the year following Hob's diagnosis, there were already signs that should have alerted me to the inevitability of new crises. In the case of mental decline, no one can anticipate what the next episode might be, the form it might take, or what one might learn from it.

The razor's edge of choice was always there—when to be concerned for him, when not. So at first I was only mildly surprised when he began to prepare for his dharma talk at the Cambridge Insight Meditation Center months before it was scheduled. The more I heard him talking about it, the more I recognized a new pattern—a lack of ease, an unfamiliar preoccupation with something so familiar.

That was how it began—one of the signature stories of Hob's last years—born from everyone's nightmare: speaking in front of a crowd and forgetting the talk you have prepared.

For years he had given talks at the meditation center. For the fateful evening, he had chosen to speak about the principle of interdependence, a core teaching of Buddhism. Many of us have a story or teaching from our spiritual tradition that we find especially inspiring. For Hob it was the image of the jeweled net of Indra, a metaphor from the Mahayana Buddhist tradition, which portrays how all beings are interconnected across time and space. The image, a vast net of interconnecting threads, describes how at all intersecting nodes there is a diamond-like jewel which represents all sentient beings—human and other—that exist in the universe. Each jewel reflects every other jewel in the vast net. Whenever suffering occurs anywhere in the great luminous net, a tear appears. In times of trouble people respond, and their compassionate response helps the net to reweave around the places of suffering. Indra's net symbolizes the principle of interbeing —the interdependence of everything in the universe.

Unlike ever before, Hob had begun making notes—and notes on notes—on this talk months in advance. He had discussed it with me. Then he had asked again about some point we'd already discussed. I was apprehensive for him.

The evening arrived. Just before I left for my commitment that night, I asked him whether he'd like me to come for support. I didn't want to suggest that I knew the talk so intimately I could have given it myself. I was still trying to support his independence. But I knew how unpredictable his ability to speak had become, especially under pressure. He declined my offer.

When I returned home later that evening, Hob appeared at the door the moment he heard my key in the lock. He was distraught. Without even greeting me, as we walked together into the family room, he began talking in a series of disconnected sentences.

"Well, it happened. I lost it. For all that preparation, I couldn't get my ideas out. I told them I'd hit the wall. I experienced a kind of terror. I haven't ever been in this place. Didn't even know it existed. I knew someday the mind would start to go, but I couldn't believe I wouldn't get any notice. I couldn't believe that this was it. I got lost in the middle of paragraphs with no strategy for this."

Without pausing in his stream of talk and very agitated, he sat down in the chair in front of the greenhouse window filled with blooming houseplants. But I noticed, too, that some of the plants had leaves that were dying back below the blossoms. Dead leaves. The death of Hob's teaching—his lifelong passion. I felt the ache in my chest as I watched him closely, tears in his eyes, his face lined with grief as he continued to pour out his experience.

"What do I do? Do I leave the room? I asked them to be patient and just kept reporting to them what was happening. I told them I had a lot to say about interbeing, that core teaching of the dharma. I told them I couldn't do the thing I had prepared. My notes were useless. Might as well have been hieroglyphics.

"Finally, I told them I knew this wasn't what they'd come for, but maybe they could stay with me as I went through this. Maybe we could meditate, and somehow I led them through a couple of guided meditations. At least I pulled that part out. But the talk. There were just some fragments. I guess you'd have to say that I experienced the death of the ego tonight—the death of pride.

"Yes, that's it. I died tonight. Now I know what it's like to die in front of a crowd of people. I don't understand why almost everyone stayed. Some of them came up afterward and said that even though the talk fell apart, they appreciated how I handled it because I told them exactly what was happening. Shared my process. I told them I have this memory problem. That it sometimes tricks me. That I'd hit the wall. But maybe we could retrieve something from the situation anyway. One woman said it was the most powerful evening she'd ever had there. Still, it was a kind of death for me."

We talked late into the night. He went over and over each part of the experience. Painstakingly, we moved through everything from his mortification to his insights. He soon recognized that this ego death had been both a painful and an inevitable part of his illness.

In the days that followed, I began to put together other pieces of that evening through the people who later spoke of it. One friend called the next day to tell me she had been sitting in the first row, close enough to feel the nuances of what he was going through. She said how riveted she was by how he handled the situation. His openness about his disabilities made it an amazing teaching for her.

"Somehow he included us in his problem," she went on. "The attention level in that room was unbelievable. It was absolutely silent. Everyone seemed to be with him. That's an evening

I will never forget. I saw what happened when a dharma teacher hits the wall, how he handled his own meltdown."

In subsequent weeks, a few other people who had been there made similar observations. It would seem that when one spoke openly about one's struggle with a problem, the openness included the people who were there. It connected everyone to what was happening, no matter how painful. It was the opposite of closing down with embarrassment or shame, for that would leave one in isolation. That apparently was one of the teachings for those who were there.

Why recount a mortifying experience? Why not excise it from memory—a failing one at that? Because what happened that night mattered so much to Hob. Because it had helped him reach a new level of acceptance toward his own process. Because it was to become one of two signature stories—each deeply revealing—of the last chapter of his life.

As with any traumatic experience, Hob kept returning to the story over and over again. Eventually for him that night was more than surviving a nightmare; it helped him to let go of some of his distress over his verbal disabilities. Even more important, it helped him accept those inevitable losses—especially the ego deaths, perhaps the most painful of all.

———— ⁕ ❦ ⁕ ————

A few days later when he was still processing the enormity of the forgotten talk, we were talking about how—even if—his years of meditation practice were helping him with these difficult situations.

"Yes, it's why it's a good idea to get your dyin' done early," he said, now able to chuckle over an expression he had used many times. "Get your dyin' done early." His words were a kind of aphorism, colloquially stated, like the Buddha's, who stated that "of all mindfulness meditations that on death is supreme."

Hob, who chronically slipped into teacher mode without realizing it, took off into what sounded like a mini dharma talk; his tendency was to share what he was currently mulling over.

"We're practicing all the time in meditation. Allowing, accepting, then letting go. Dyin' early. How early? How soon? How about the next breath. Get in the habit of letting go. I sure wouldn't have chosen to go through what happened that night, but it sure helped me with my dying. It's hard because we're always in a hurry to get out of the hard stuff—the hard mood states. We don't want to get rid of all the strong feelings we have and be a holy blob. The practice is about how we transform those difficult energies. First we have to let them all be. Then we can stop and just let go and die a little. We don't want to miss our appointment with life."

Some months earlier T. T., our friend the Tibetan tulku, had asked Hob how was his meditation practice now that he was dealing with mental loss? Hob had answered, "Whatever I do, that's it, because I don't know how many more 'its' they're going to be. There's a deepening acceptance not only of yourself, but of your place in life. It's very nice to be old. There isn't as long a vista into the future, especially because my mind is taking an early lunch break."

The three of us laughed. Hob was speaking with such lightness about a potentially devastating subject that I couldn't help but feel a sense of rejoicing for him. It was his nature to soften the sharp edges of any difficult situation. Another gift of the journey.

Hand in hand, we had walked home from T.T.'s along a quiet, tree-lined street in our neighborhood. I was looking out for the irregular places in the sidewalks where the roots of trees heaved the bricks into undulating terrain, treacherous for walkers. Vigilance had become the rule whenever I accompanied him anywhere. I feared for his stumbling or falling, because experience had shown that he was no longer as aware of the physical perils around him.

He continued to muse about the earlier conversation as if it had never ended. "It's different—this having to slow down. But it's not grim," he said. "It's not about just accepting this new world of 'slowth,' but enjoying it! Lightness and spaciousness and humor are what it's about.

"A final legacy to the world—at least mine—will be to be happy, to pass on the tendency to enjoy—not just Christmas Eve, but the ordinary times. This mental loss thing is nature's way of saying, 'Stop, be quiet. Don't give me so much to chew on mentally.'"

And then he ironically concluded:

"My solemn obligation is to be happy!"

One late afternoon about three years after the diagnosis, I climbed the stairs to the third floor to wake Hob from an unusually long nap. By this time waking Hob from oversleeping had become a familiar ritual—climb the stairs, open the door, walk into the soft light of the room, and never know what state of mind he might be in.

"There's something's that's happened," he said as he lay on the daybed at the far end of the room. His inexplicit language told me that he was in another realm. My awareness shifted; I was alert as someone waiting for thunder after a sharp flash of lightning.

"Is it like being a stranger in a strange land?" I asked. He nodded.

"It must be weird to be with someone . . ." He started the sentence, then stopped. He was dreamy, disconnected, distant. He kept trying to talk as if we were having a regular conversation.

"Everything will be okay," he said. I'd learned that this was his code phrase to reassure me that, at some level, something was still okay. It suggested that he still had some thread of awareness about what was happening, even if he couldn't find words to express it. Another pause.

"Are you going away?" he asked.

"No, I'm going to stay right here. I'm not going anywhere, even downstairs, until we've unscrambled things a bit."

His eyes filled with tears and he reached up to pull me down into a hug.

"I feel really alone. I'm here but I don't know where. Where are we?"

"I think you've had another episode where something's happened in some part of your brain. But remember, other times when that's happened after your nap, you've had something to eat. Food and time seem to help. But it must be scary for you."

"Yes, it's really strange." Pause. "Is everyone okay?" How quickly his concern for others surfaced.

"Yes, as far as I know."

"This is really strange. Everything's going to be okay."

"Yes, I think it will, and maybe a snack would be a good idea for now."

I felt that these few exchanges had helped him to feel some reconnection with me and ordinary reality. It was possible to coax him downstairs, to change the environs as one might do with a troubled child.

How presumptuous of us to assume that we live in a stable reality! We construct reality to negotiate our way through life, but that ceases to be true for someone living with dementia. Or for me, his partner in this journey. I had to join Hob in ricocheting between the ordinary and the non-ordinary.

The next day he continued to be more disoriented than usual. He couldn't distinguish between the refrigerator and the freezer. He started to look for something, like the matches, but opened the wrong drawer. I ached for him. I ached for myself. Each of his losses felt like someone had hit me in the solar plexus. We're going to make it, I'd reassure myself, but sometimes I wondered how.

As I was leading Hob down the back stairs after our delicate post-nap exchange, I glanced out the window at the majestic elm tree that we so loved. For a moment, I tried to absorb its quiet strength and flexible grace. As we descended—very slowly, very carefully, one step at a time, holding hands so I could steady Hob's uncertain gait—I was transported back to the company of trees I'd known in my childhood. In a flash, it seemed, I went from looking out at the elm tree outside our house in Cambridge to "Lawn Cottage," the place where I lived as a little girl on Long Island.

In many ways, it was an idyllic place to grow up. Our rented cottage, one of many on a sprawling estate, was across the road from a huge expanse of lawn graced with trees—elms, oaks, and my favorite, the weeping beech whose branches came all the way to the ground so we could crawl inside and be hidden in a bower of green and gold light. For the kids who lived on the estate, the formal garden was one of our favorite places to play. The main entrance to the garden led through a wooden entryway and down broad brick steps to a fountain at the bottom of the garden. With its long hedges, hemlock bowers, and trellises overflowing with orange trumpet vine, the garden was a paradise for the kids to play hide-and-seek. Scurrying to my favorite hiding place, I'd climb into one of the huge terracotta urns that stood at the top of the main stairway into the garden. For me, the urn was shoulder height. I would put my hands onto the sun-warmed rim at the top, crawl up its rounded sides, and snuggle down into the damp dark to hide, never, I hoped, to be found. I didn't mind that I had to part the spider webs and urge the scurrying little creatures away from my perch. Then I'd guide myself into exquisite silence.

"Be very still," I'd tell myself. "Quiet. Even quieter so the others won't find me."

Then I'd hear the footsteps coming closer. My friend who was "it" slapped the side of the urn with his hand as he walked by. He shattered the silence, startling me out of my quiet state. But he didn't look in.

Minutes passed. More precious silence. Time to dream. I loved the solitude of my earthen womb, warm with summer sun. I felt comforted and protected by the moist dark. This was my secret place, my private little kingdom.

"Alli, alli, in-free! Alli, alli, in-free!" the boy called out across the garden. I crawled out, wiping spider webs from my hair, triumphant that no one had discovered my secret place.

Suddenly I was wrenched out of my childhood reveries by the sound of Hob's voice. We were nearly at the bottom of the stairs when he squeezed my hand harder and asked, "Where did you say we were going? To have some tea? I need something to eat. I'm still feeling strange. I think I've lost something."

"That's okay," I responded. "We'll get you something—maybe those cream-filled ginger cookies that you love. I know some sugar helps in the late afternoon when your energy is low."

He settled down at the family room table and gazed absently out the glass doors to our bird feeder, invariably the scene of squirrel antics. At the moment, two squirrels seemed content to be foraging around on the ground under the feeder, retrieving a feast of discarded birdseed.

As I moved on automatic pilot around the kitchen, putting on the kettle, arranging cookies on a plate, wiping the counter, I couldn't seem to let go of the childhood memories that had come to me so forcefully as we'd descended the stairs. I mechanically wiped up the post-lunch stains on the counter. As my hand wiped in rhythmic circular patterns across the counter, I found myself back with more childhood images, remembering the vast lawn with its grand trees and how carefree I felt as a five-year-old in that beautiful place. That little girl seemed to be prodding my memory to remember something important, but what was it? Then it came to me—a time when I'd been in a personal growth workshop. We'd been led through a guided imagery session in which we were invited to go back in time and meet ourselves as children.

In the imagery session, I had found myself back on the great lawn across the road from our cottage. I was barefoot, as I usually was on a warm, timeless, summer day. I walked toward the cluster of miniature Japanese maple trees at the far corner of the lawn, another of my favorite hideouts. I crawled under their feathered leaves, looked up to their silvery bark and curving, graceful limbs which created a protected, magical bower.

At this point in the imagery session, we were invited to see a child of our own age walking toward us. I saw a little girl about five years old in the distance. She was walking up the sheep meadow toward me. She climbed over the post-and-rail fence that separated the lawn from the field, and when she got to the top, she stopped and looked toward me. Our eyes met.

Tall for her age and slender, she was barefoot and dressed in a yellow and white striped T-shirt and bright red shorts. She had strikingly blue eyes, and her blond hair, so light it looked almost like spun gold, was braided into two pigtails that bounced as she walked. She was happy in her little body, but as I gazed longer at those eyes, I saw a combination of curiosity, wonder, and inwardness—as if she needed to protect something.

Vaguely I began to realize that she was my double—myself as a five-year-old girl. As she kept walking slowly toward me, I knew that she was approaching to give me some kind of special message. She stopped in front of me, stood silently for several moments, then spoke in a young voice that surprised me with its authority.

"Be free," she said. "Be free. That is my message for you."

Still deep in these memories of childhood, I was surprised by the prickling of tears that her message released in me. As I poured the boiling water into the mugs, I knew my tears were those of recognition—of being seen and known at a deep level. Tears awakened by the simple wisdom of a child—myself as a child—the one who knew my love of secret, inner worlds, the one who knew the longing of the soul to be free.

⸺ ❦ ⸺

Childhood memories, fantasies of hiding or escaping to idyllic places, these moments were hardly a surprise given the increasing responsibilities of caregiving. Yet the strain and sadness of our situation were counterbalanced by Hob's wit and drive to lighten situations, including the craziness of his own mental losses.

"You've got to have a few laughs. That's the main thing. That's my contribution to the world."

Hob's unique sense of humor was his greatest ally. On a beautiful day when he couldn't find the book he'd been reading, he said, "I feel as though someone has taken the wheels off my roller skates!" Then, his infectious laugh.

Or, another moment when he couldn't recall something, he declared, "I disremembered that!" quoting from Amos and Andy, a radio program from the 1940s and '50s. "Now *they* had the right word for it!"

Hob used to make fun of his obsession with words, his determination to correct people's grammar, and the tirelessness of his editorial pen. With macabre delight, he once constructed an imaginary scene of his own execution, where in the last moments as he climbed the steps to the gallows he would be preoccupied with rewriting his own death sentence!

In these days of his growing limitation, when he couldn't find some word he wanted, he started playing with any words that were around.

"There is more madness in my method than method in my madness!"

He kept turning the unpredictability of Alzheimer's into one comical statement after another. In fact, his credo was that we needed to spend a certain amount of time laughing each day. That reminded me of a startling exchange from several years earlier when we were at Plum Village in the south of France for the summer retreat with Thich Nhat Hanh, the Zen teacher and peace activist.

"Do you remember, Hob, that historic exchange you had with Joan at Plum Village a couple of years ago?"

He looked perplexed. Clearly he didn't remember.

I started to recreate the scene for him. We had decided to go for a walk. We followed the path through the front meadow in the Upper Hamlet of the Plum Village complex and noticed a fig tree covered with ripe fruit. In the distance we could see fields of sunflowers awash with yellow radiance. The sunflower fields, abundant in that part of France, alternated in orderly patterns with rolling hills of vineyards, each with its own farm lying protected in the valley. The air was sweet with the smells of summer, and there was a gentle breeze that made the leaves dance with light.

"Remember how beautiful it was, the first sunny day after all those cold, raw days with nothing but rain and fog?"

"Oh, yes," he chimed in. "It was 'lazy day,' that day in the week we had off from the usual schedule, did nothing much."

"Right, and we couldn't resist the temptation of picking

those figs."

We had parted the branches to find ourselves inside the tree's canopy, in a light-filled bower created by the branches that came down to the ground in a green embrace around us. With great care, stepping around branches, reaching high for the figs, we filled our backpack, not just for the walk but to have snacks back in our room.

We emerged from the fig tree just in time to see Joan, one of Hob's fellow dharma teachers, walking along the road at the edge of the meadow. As we called out, she turned and started in our direction. Judging from her stride, she had some agenda in mind. After accepting a handful of figs from us, evidently eager to get to the business at hand, she said, "Okay Hob, I want to ask you something. I've been asked to be the guest editor for an issue of *Tricycle* magazine (a Buddhist quarterly) that will deal with the subject of Death and Dying. You're probably familiar with that section where various practitioners are all asked the same question. We print your answer next to your photograph. I can get someone around here to take it.

"So here's my question to you: If you were able to write your own script, if you were able to create all the circumstances you wanted . . ." she paused, "how would you like to die?"

A flicker of a smile crossed Hob's face and without a moment's hesitation, he replied, "I'd like to die laughing!"

Amidst our laughter at his answer, I realized that besides being humorous about a weighty subject, it was entirely consistent with his nature and similar to remarks he'd made before.

Yet his response certainly shook up any concepts about how to view one's own death.

Later, during a discouraged moment or when Hob raised the subject of his death, I would remind him of what he had said.

Earlier in the retreat, Hob had told Joan about his memory problems, how he was already struggling for words and anxious about his future teaching. She had replied simply, "You're a blessing without any dharma talks. You're an elder in our community. And what you are living through—this is the ultimate here and now experience."

We would occasionally return to her message; it was a reminder that after all the years of practicing meditation to retrain the mind to dwell in the present moment, brain disease gradually leaves you unable to recall the past or plan for the future. "The ultimate here and now" would become a touch-point for us both along the way. I titled my writing file with those words.

⸺ ⸎ ⸺

There was the laughter, and there were the precipices of life. Neither of us knew when we'd find ourselves at the next edge, either of laughter or of free fall. If I hadn't had the thread of practice to hold on to, I don't know how I would have managed. Countless times, I needed to anchor myself with the next breath. I needed to feel the solidity of my body, instead of spinning off into thoughts and feelings which would sabotage the equanimity that Hob's situation demanded. I had to keep coming home to myself. If I didn't, I would get lost in the complexity of so many demanding moments.

One windy fall evening, we were quietly reading after dinner when I noticed with some concern that he had found my copy of *Alzheimer's: A Caregiver's Guide*. I noticed that he was reading, in the later chapters of the book, a description of the late stages of the disease. He looked up from the pages.

"No one in their right mind would ever want to live like this. There must be a pill you can take. The question is, how do you know when it's time to go?"

We were on the next precipice. Several times over the three years since his diagnosis, he had brought up the subject of death. It was a subject about which he was exceptionally open; his years of teaching and meditation naturally had deepened his understanding of death. He had also worked with Hospice and taught a course on Death and Dying at a local college.

Thus began our first long conversation about how to die, if one were going to make that awesome choice. I began to recount a story from my family about how my great-grandmother had died. When she was in her early nineties, she had reached a point where her health was rapidly breaking down. She decided to eat less, maybe fast, although the story was vague about this. The story made it clear that she had decided to die.

One evening she called her family around her. Sherry was served—so the story goes—and then she announced her intention. There must have been a moment of shock, maybe disbelief, maybe even protest. She was portrayed, however, as a determined, strong woman, so perhaps no family member questioned her decision. There was reminiscing. There were tears and laughter. There were last words. She retired to bed and the next morning she was gone.

None of us can know exactly what happened, but apparently she had called upon their trusted family doctor for assistance. Given her age and weakened condition, he may have helped her to carry out her wish to die.

Hob was intrigued with the story. It was clear how much he needed to talk about ways of dying. We went back to the time when our friends, the owners of the local bookstore, had been reading *Final Exit*, the Hemlock Society publication which had precipitated a lively discussion about the subject of death. But I didn't tell Hob that someone had recently loaned me a copy of the book. I found it so distressing that I placed it back on the shelf. I prayed that I wouldn't have to look at this topic for a long, long time, if ever. I accepted my own ambivalence, knowing that I was caught between belief systems. In the Eastern traditions, taking one's life, even in the late stages of terminal illness, is regarded as interfering with natural destiny. Then there was my great-grandmother, respected in our family for her courage and the grace with which she followed through.

This conversation had a dreamlike quality to it. I couldn't imagine how I could be so detached, or how Hob's scenario might play out. So I listened to him and responded as if we were talking about plans for our next vacation.

"We're going to need help and support with this one," I said as the conversation wound down. I knew that the critical factor was his awareness. This disease quietly devours a person's awareness, creating a gap here, a hole there. With awareness comes choice; when awareness goes, choice goes.

"We can call in Charles to be the point man," he said later when we were lying in bed in the dark. Charles, for whom Hob had been a mentor, was a beloved friend. I was astonished at how dramatically his mood had shifted from his earlier heaviness to the possibility that he could choose a way out. He even sounded upbeat, like someone who had just discovered a new trip to take.

"I'll go ahead and explore the next chapter," he said, "and prepare the way for you."

THE CHALLENGES OF MENTAL LOSS
Reflections

* The process of mental loss is one of the most agonizing aspects of this illness. For everyone it's a procession of shock, disbelief, and pain. The stark reality of what's happening requires us to keep accepting and letting go, although we may simultaneously be grief stricken and enraged at the injustices of the illness. We start to realize that we are living in a world of extremes—a test of our energy and endurance—something that is helpful to acknowledge.

* In the presence of mental loss, we learn to live in constantly shifting realities, ricocheting between the ordinary and non-ordinary, between sense and non-sense. This may be one of the most difficult challenges we've ever dealt with; it demands openness, steadiness, flexibility, and compassion. Appreciate that it's also tiring and heartrending.

* Realize that you may need to become something of an archaeologist, ever in search of meanings in the increasingly confused language of the patient. We also need to be citadels of patience as we listen time and again to the same question or phrase or story. Our presence is their anchor to a disappearing world.

Hard as it is, we are invited over and over again to stay present to what is difficult. That becomes our practice, our life, our gift to the patient. We are living, as our friend said, in "the ultimate here and now." Finally, certain qualities are being called forth in us, such as steadfastness and compassion. We are in a fire of initiation into the most difficult chapter of our lives.

* As we witness all the losses, it's possible that we may start to distance ourselves emotionally from the patient. Our fears are at least twofold. First, we're shaken by the stream of losses, as well as by the feelings triggered in us—our fear of this process and how it might unfold.

Secondly, although we may not recognize it, we may be anxious for ourselves: What if this happens to me? We may start to objectify the patient, see her mainly as someone with a disease, or talk about her in the third person in her presence as if she weren't there. The mind may be going, but there is more to us than the mind. However we make sense of this complex subject, the patient is always worthy of our love and respect, regardless of the state of their mind.

* Everyone handles the onset of a major illness in a unique way. My mother never spoke of it, perhaps because she chose not to or because she could not. Hob, however, spoke about it a lot. He put people at their ease because he was so open. Embarrassment and shame often make people shut down in silence. Silence, however, is perplexing, uncomfortable, and distancing. It's the elephant-in-the-room syndrome; it spins everyone into a web of avoidance and discomfort. If we simply name what's going on, we include others in our situation and create connection instead of isolation.

* Faced with so much unpredictability, I had to keep returning to the breath as my anchor; be aware of my body; stay open, present, and conscious of whatever might arise. This is the practice of presence—a spiritual practice recognized by many religious traditions. This

helps give meaning to what can seem like a hopeless or meaningless task.

Suggestions

∗ As you deal with the unspoken questions of friends and community, find some simple sentence that explains the situation, one that demystifies it. You can say something as simple as, "My wife/husband/parent is dealing with memory problems."

∗ Whenever we bring playfulness or humor into a difficult situation, it lightens everything up. Can you find ways to do this that fit your circumstances? Hob's statement was a great example of this: "My solemn obligation is to be happy." Then you can recall or return to these lighter moments as a way to uplift things.

∗ Realize how you have become the facilitator of conversations; find ways to include the one with Alzheimer's in the conversation even if she is quite impaired. Remember that physical touch is one of the sweetest ways to keep them included.

Seed Thoughts

My presence alone is a gift.

Let me find ways to bring lightness to our situation.

May I stay open, flexible, and caring.

115

CHAPTER FIVE
YOU CAN'T MESS WITH BACH

It was an unlikely way for two people to meet. And it was equally unlikely that eventually four people would meet and become close friends. One evening about ten years before Hob began to show signs of memory loss, he was sitting around reading the alumni notes in *Harvard Magazine*, an odd activity since he hadn't even graduated from that university. True, he'd spent a year as a visiting scholar at Harvard when we first moved to Cambridge, and then another year at the Divinity School when he was making a career change into the field of psychology and counseling. Nevertheless, that evening he was perusing the stories of Harvard graduates—all strangers to him—when he stumbled across a story that riveted his attention.

He walked into the kitchen and launched into an animated account of his discovery.

"I just read an unbelievable story in this alumni magazine," he said, as he leaned back against the counter watching me stir spices and vegetables together in an Indian curry.

"You won't believe what this guy did. First of all, he's writing from jail. Have you got that—a Harvard graduate writing notes to the alumni magazine from his prison cell. That got my attention! Seems he's a big-time peace activist who's been involved in a number of civil disobedience actions.

"But this time, he goes to Draper Labs, you know, the place right here in Cambridge that designs missile systems for U.S. nuclear warheads. And what does he do? At eight o'clock in the morning, he walks into the lobby of Draper when everyone is coming in to work, and he releases a cage full of white doves. Can you imagine the chaos—white doves flying all around the lobby of this heavy-duty defense industry! What do you suppose happened and how did they ever catch those doves? That's so far out!"

"So what happened after that?" I asked, thoroughly intrigued.

"Obviously he got arrested. He landed in jail for awhile. I don't know for how long, but this guy really intrigues me. Apparently he lives with his wife at Haley House, the Catholic Worker house in the South End, which has a soup kitchen for serving the homeless. It takes me back to the early days in New York when I was involved in the social justice work. I'm going to look this guy up, find out what he's up to now."

"What's his name?" I asked.

"His name's Jim Levinson—the Harvard inmate." He laughed and shook his head with disbelief.

Indeed, soon after, we did met Jim and his wife Louise. Jim, with his ebullient spiritedness, not only found time to organize protests against defense industries but also turned out to be a consummate musician and Tufts professor who traveled frequently to the Middle East and Asia as a nutrition consultant. Louise, with her ready laugh and easy presence, seemed like a calming anchor to Jim's oceanic personality. She had perhaps the most varied spiritual biography of anyone I knew: raised a Presbyterian, she converted to Catholicism, then practiced Tibetan Buddhism, studied the Enneagram, astrology, and Tarot, and to top it all was married to Jim who eventually became a *shaliach tzibur*, meaning "messenger of the people," for the synagogue in Brattleboro, Vermont, near where they eventually moved.

And so a rare friendship unfolded from Hob's random moment with an alumni magazine. The four of us stayed close through the next lively chapter of their lives, when they moved to the country west of Boston to start a communal farm to provide fresh vegetables for the Haley House soup kitchen. That was when Jim started the Noonday Singers, of which Hob was a member. The group traveled around the East Coast performing their songs of hope and struggle.

After ten years at the farm, Jim and Louise moved back into Cambridge. Jim, an inveterate force for creating community, brought together what we informally called our family spiritual group. We started to meet several years before Hob's diagnosis. The group was made up of four couples, ranging in age from thirty to seventy-five, Hob being the elder of our group. We met every six to eight weeks. We were eight people seeking community by coming together to share food, singing, and discussion on topics that touched deeper dimensions of our lives. We celebrated the holidays—the holy days—from different traditions: Succoth and Rosh Hashanah to Christmas and Passover. Over the four years we had been meeting, we became a deeply bonded group that occasionally included our children.

Only a few days after Hob and I had had our first serious conversation about the subject of death, the group convened at our house. It was the first time after the summer. Everyone knew that Hob's health was slipping. He was becoming ever quieter at our gatherings. What they didn't know, however, was that in the last few days he and I had been living with the Himalayan question of how to die if one chooses to end life. Neither of us had any idea where it might lead. I harbored my own questions: What was my responsibility in this? What might my role be? Would he ask me to help or support his decision in some way?

We began the evening with a potluck dinner, then lingered at the dining room table to sing some of our favorite music, from a sorrowful lament in Hebrew to "Jubilate Deo," an exuberant Latin round. Filled with good food and music, we moved into our living room for discussion.

The curtains were drawn against the cool night as we lit the fire which radiated warmth and dancing light into the room. The light flickered on the Haitian painting over the couch, a colorful painting of dancers that Hob had brought back from the summer he'd led a work camp in Haiti. In the middle of our circle on a low table was a simple altar of autumn leaves and three candles that burned brightly. There was a sense of deep quiet, of anticipation. Because Rosh Hashanah was near, our topic for the evening was "transitions."

Surprisingly, for he rarely spoke first, Hob began to speak.

"I've been having some pretty heavy thoughts lately." He stopped for a moment.

"Thoughts about how maybe it's time for me to get off the bus."

A long pause. No one spoke.

"It's getting really hard, and I guess the time comes when it's just not worth it anymore."

Where were we going to go from there? I was astonished at Hob's openness. He had cast this weighty issue out of the silence into the middle of our circle. What followed was, for each of us in different ways, a rare opening to the great issue of death. He had reached out in a great leap of faith. Each person responded to him in their unique way. There were tears and laughter. Susan told him what an inspiration he had been to her, how his attitude toward his illness was helping her to deal with her own father's decline.

There was Elise's eloquent expression of her love for Hob, her father-in-law. With tears streaming down her face, she rose from her chair in front of the fire and crossed the circle to embrace Hob. Barely able to form words through her tears, she kept speaking, then stopping.

"There's no way to tell you how much you mean to me. . . . How you've supported me . . . encouraged me. . . . I can't bear hearing you talk this way. . . . I couldn't bear to lose you. . . .

I don't want you going anywhere."

Hob was in tears, too. At that moment, the love in the room was boundless and all-embracing. As I sat there, love and sadness were spiraling through my body in a wild dance, making it difficult to draw the next breath. I wasn't sure what was the greatest relief—the tears that overflowed or everyone's loving support. The room was vibrant with life even as we were speaking about death.

Then there was our son's response. Ethan leaned forward in his chair, his tall, lanky frame in a tense posture. He looked troubled. His brow was furrowed. His blue eyes were intense. Ever the one to be bold and honest and outspoken, now his voice was charged with intensity.

"Dad, I get upset and angry when you talk about this. I feel as though it's way too soon to be thinking about it. It seems like it's your unilateral response to the Alzheimer's. I want you to stay around. I want us to keep our family whole for as long as possible, and for you to be a grandfather to our boys, so they'll know you and remember you."

Now the silence felt electric. Hob sat still next to me on the couch. Finally he spoke.

"Thanks, Eth. I'm glad you said how you feel about all this. I guess I'll just have to keep mulling this one over. Just don't know now . . ." His sentence tapered off.

Clearly Hob was deeply touched, maybe also surprised, by everyone's response to his momentous question about death. By the time we stood in a circle, arms around one another's shoulders, to bring the evening to a close, the feeling had once again shifted into lightness and merriment. It felt as though we had all been through an initiation, where Hob had invited us to ponder with him the great koan of death, to plunge into the deepest places of love and pain.

He expressed relief that the group had supported him by listening and responding, and said that would stay with him beyond the meeting. I shared in his relief, for his questions about death were no longer confined to the two of us.

Later that evening after everyone had headed out into the brisk night, Ethan called back to clarify what he had said. He explained to Hob that it had been difficult for him to express his feelings. It was true he'd felt anger and dismay, but now he wanted his father to know that he would also honor his wishes and respect any decision that he made.

As Ethan concluded in that last conversation of the evening, "Dad, you know better than anyone when the right time is. We'll support you in whatever feels right to you. You may know something that we don't know. It wouldn't be quitting. It would be tremendously courageous."

———

Extraordinary as our family group meeting had been, all of us could sense that Hob needed more time for discussion than he'd had. The issue was too complex for us to struggle with alone. So we agreed to meet the next day with Jimmy and Louise to continue the discussion.

The next morning the four of us were back together. The living room was bright with sunlight, while the backyard, visible through the sliding glass doors, was radiant with fall color and late blooming flowers. Near the beginning of our meeting with Jim and Louise, Hob, as he was still apt to do, encapsulated the essence of why we'd gathered by quoting one of his poetic fragments.

"Life and death upon one tether, and running beautiful together."[1] He spoke with relish, heartened, I was sure, that he could still provide a wise perspective on this difficult topic.

Louise thought it was important that we reaffirm what I had been calling the "meta level" of our situation, a term she'd heard me use often enough that it had become part of my lexicon. As I saw it, we needed to frame this difficult time of our lives in the largest perspective—as part of our soul agreement as a couple. This perspective could only be speculative—a port in a storm that protected us when the going got really rough. But it helped.

All couples obviously have powerful karma with each other—shared destinies. How could it be an accident, then, that part of our destiny was to share the experience of this disease? This was our challenge: to see how we could transform suffering by learning what it was trying to teach us, no matter how hard or harrowing the lessons might be. The call was to be open, to share as much as we could. What we were learning would help us and, hopefully, others as well. Whenever I reminded Hob about the meta level of our situation—the broader perspective—it helped both of us through many difficult passages. It allowed me to trust in the natural order of things, for amidst all that was hard there were also many moments of grace. Even blessings. As the Taoist tradition says: "The ten thousand joys and the ten thousand sorrows."

The turning point of our meeting was when Jim invited us to assess the quality of life, given Hob's accelerating losses.

"How much pleasure and meaning do you derive from life and give to others?" he asked Hob. "That is an indicator. It seems to all of us that you are getting a lot of pleasure from life and giving a lot as well. In fact, I think you give a lot more than you're aware of. That's your challenge, Hob! You don't see or appreciate how deeply and lightly, with humor, you touch people. You can't be the judge of that!"

We all laughed at the way Jim was speaking to Hob, high-lighting an issue most of us share—the tendency to underplay our own gifts. For indeed, how do any of us know, even remotely, when or how we touch the lives of others?

"You know what I think, Hob? The person who's going to decide this for you is Johann Sebastian Bach!"

Immediately there was a sense of expectancy among the four of us. What was Jim getting at? He had a mischievous expression as he continued.

"Your love of music, Hob, is enormous, so the appreciation and sharing of music should be central in your life. As long as that's here, you stay! Bach would never allow anyone to get off the bus while they were deriving so much pleasure from his music. He simply wouldn't permit it! And you can't mess with Bach!"

We all laughed at the enjoyment of having Bach as an arbiter in this matter. Jim went on.

"So, I think this is one indicator to keep an eye on. You need to allow yourself to receive and take everything in, whether it's music, friendship, love, or whatever. Remember how much you've given to others. You've been a teacher, a healer, always pouring out to other people. And you know how much pleasure and nourishment that's given you. Now it's time for you to let others do that for you. If it's hard for you, you've got to bite your tongue and learn to live with it! Words aren't that important in any of your close relationships, and besides, words are secondary with Bach, too!"

Hob was chuckling now, but I also sensed his discomfort.

"I guess my biggest fear is of being a nuisance," he said, well aware of the stress I'd been under and feeling responsible for it.

"If you feel like you're being a nuisance, Hob," Jim replied, "then you're going to have to learn to live with those feelings, too: letting people care for you, learning to receive. Consider all this a spiritual discipline! And furthermore, if you have trouble finding the words, or find yourself at some kind of a loss, consider that a spiritual discipline, too!"

We all laughed. Jim had a way of making the most difficult circumstances seem manageable, even humorous. Then Hob spoke, and I could see from his expression that something unexpected and probably humorous was coming.

"Per ardua ad astra," he said, articulating each word carefully then ending with a flourish.

"Whoa, Hob! What does that one mean?" someone asked.

"Through hardship to the stars," he replied.

The Latin aphorism came from some distant corner of his classical education. I realized that this expression was close in spirit to Nietzsche's saying, one I sometimes invoked when one of us was going through a tumultuous time:

"You must become a chaos to give birth to a dancing star."

Louise brought us back to where we had started, specifically to Hob's original image.

"So, Hob, what are we going to do about this image of 'getting off the bus?' After all we've talked about this morning, I think it needs to change. The wisdom traditions speak about death as a transition from one state to another, so maybe it's more like getting a transfer!" More laughter.

"Come to think of it," she continued, "the slaves had it right when they talked about 'free at last,' which was more about the ultimate freedom than about freedom from slavery. That's freedom of the soul, the ultimate freedom."

"I'm flirting with the inarticulable," Hob replied.

His statement, freighted with possible meanings, struck me as another of his encoded messages. Of course his words were slipping away, leaving him with the "inarticulable." But recently, especially upon waking in the morning, he had also been in touch with the ineffable—inner states where everything had fallen into place, charged with clarity. In these moments he felt complete, in a state of supreme well-being. He called these experiences moments of grace.

As the meeting ended, we acknowledged how valuable it had been to talk so openly. It wasn't about making any decisions at this point; it was about our process of living with Alzheimer's. And about trusted friends who could help us to handle something so controversial and charged.

As Hob said, with panache, at the end of the meeting, "It's a privilege to be in this close. We will speak of death and we will sing!"

We agreed to meet again whenever necessary, and given that singing was one of our common bonds, we would be sure to frame the meeting with song.

We both felt tremendously heartened and buoyed up by these two events—the family group evening and the meeting with Jim and Louise. Through the deepening mists of Hob's mental diminishment, he had called out for help. He and I could feel in a tangible, intimate way how this circle of family and friends were now standing with us in our journey. It was an extraordinary gift; we felt as if we'd been wrapped round with protection and hopefulness. Hob wasn't to speak of death again for almost a year.

When we're healthy, we use our capabilities without giving them much thought. Self-motivation, choice, and will govern our lives effortlessly, but these seemed like miraculous gifts to me as I watched them erode in Hob's world. He was reaching that point where choice became incapacitated, where will disintegrated, where life drifted aimlessly.

One windy fall afternoon while we were working outside in Vermont, I noticed that he was still holding the same clutch of sticks he had picked up off the lawn almost half an hour earlier. I could see that he meant to take them to the kindling barrel, but somewhere between that initial intention and its implementation, his mental circuitry had disconnected. Did he know the sticks were in his hand? Was he quietly anxious about some lost thought, or was that just my projection? He appeared content in his objectless meanderings around the yard. When I suggested that perhaps he'd like to take the sticks into the living room, he brightened and said, "Oh yes, I was meaning to but got sidetracked."

Life now seemed to be one sidetrack following another. *Ah, the gift of intention,* I thought to myself as I watched him. We take it for granted that we can hold an intention long enough to act, but for him that gift had been impaired in tiny increments. Imperceptibly, the balance had shifted toward disability. Suddenly, over just one weekend, I was staggered by the differences.

"What are we going to do today?" he had asked several times that morning. In the past, he rarely asked that question. Now it reverberated between us. He was signaling, "I'm not sure what to do next. Where should I be? Where am I supposed to go?"

What must it be like to live in a world of uncertainties,

where nothing beckons, where one moment slides into the next with ease, like a piece of flotsam on the stream, carried by the current with no will of its own?

Even more dismaying, I noticed that he hadn't fed the fish in our pond. Ever since his father had taught him to fish as a boy, he'd had a love for these finned creatures that filled me with wonder. True fishermen will understand. He went into a deep reverie whenever he approached a stream, searching the shady corners of pools for a slim, dark shape languorously swimming in the currents. For him, fish held an almost mystical fascination, a symbolic theme that wove its way through his life. In turn, he'd taught our son Ethan to fish, one of the deepest ways that they'd connected as father and son.

When I first knew him, he had said humorously, but also with a dash of seriousness, that his life would feel complete if we lived by a pond with trout in it. And so we'd figured out a way at our place in Vermont to cycle water from our stream with an ingenious gravity system to create a pond and stock it with trout. He was the lover and master overseer of that pond; he stocked it each spring, tended its edges, treated it for algae, and cared for the forty or so fish that inhabited it as if they were his children in nature.

At the end of day, his ritual was to feed the trout. He stood for long, ruminative periods as he threw trout food over the darkening waters, watching the play of fish as they rose, sometimes barely dimpling the surface of the water, other times swirling and leaping in wild feeding frenzies. Hob stood, a solitary figure, utterly content, as he watched the dance of pond life.

Now he no longer remembered to feed the fish. How sad that something he loved so passionately had slipped away. No fish were rising for their food; the surface of the pond was left quiet.

In the twilight I felt sadness—for Hob, for his losses, for the life we once had, all slipping away. But then in contrast, out of nowhere a sweet memory arose of another late afternoon by the pond.

Hob, wearing his old faded green fishing vest with all its pockets, was standing slightly behind our son Ethan who held a trout rod tentatively in his hands—a fishing lesson at dusk. Hob was showing him how to hold the rod with a delicate touch, to sense the faintest movement at the end of the line. Everything about that moment was in Hob's posture—the protective leaning of his body, the hands teaching by touch, the tender attention of a father to a son as he learned a new skill.

I remembered the fishing lesson scene, but then in lively contrast, I had other flashbacks to the titanic struggles between father and son, two strong-willed personalities set against one another. As a little boy Ethan had come roaring into life filled with fire. He loved drama and if something wasn't happening, he jolly well made it happen!

On the other hand, Hob, who became a parent for the first time in his early forties, sometimes found parenting a challenge. He had a tendency to be excessively judgmental with both Ethan and our daughter, Laura, which was a source of contention between Hob and me and the cause of innumerable flash points in our family. With Hob's criticisms and Ethan's hair-trigger temper, they were two angry people facing off in competition. That's how Ethan described it as an adult. Hob's intensity and fire were subterranean; Ethan's exploded outward. I took on the role of mediator, while Laura's response was to vanish to her room.

And so, like many a family, we struggled with our frightful scenes. Sometimes Hob and I wondered how we would make it through the parenting chapter of our lives. We tried everything! There were Hob's and my endless powwows, haphazard family meetings, parent effectiveness training, visits to family therapists—alone, together, and all four of us. Somehow we survived those tumultuous early years to become a very close-knit family.

Perhaps it was fishing as much as anything that finally solidified the bond between Hob and Ethan. They went off on several fishing trips to distant places, just the two of them out in the wilderness. Fishing was an initiation, a ritual, a male bonding.

Memory softens the rougher edges of life so we can begin to laugh at the hardest of memories. I could now appreciate the richness of our family life together and how many really tough challenges we'd worked through over the years. For that I was grateful, especially now that we were facing this most difficult chapter of our life as a family.

As I watched the process of deterioration of Hob's mind, I was determined to understand as best I could what he was going through. I observed his changing mind-states like a detective. Rather than dismiss the troubling signs as hopeless or deplorable, I wondered what clues might be hidden there. How could I help him shift the difficult moments of loss or confusion into something lighter? How could I help him let go of frustration, encourage him toward more ease? I had no formula. Every situation was different. Sometimes it wasn't possible because he became locked into some pattern, a strange stubbornness he'd never had that I couldn't break into. Then I resorted to touching, hugging, or leading him away from the source of frustration—the very tactics one uses with a child.

Unlike most other ventures in my life where I'd steeped myself in the literature or training around some subject, I chose not to submerge myself in the literature on Alzheimer's disease. I had read several of the key books, owned a caretaker's guide, and took an excellent course on Rehabilitation Therapy, the current approach to management of the disease. But I felt cautioned by the power of conditioning, having learned that if you absorb the perspectives of others you can end up living the opinions, paradigms, and predictions of other people rather than the truth of the situation before you. Maybe this was a subtle form of denial on my part, but I felt a resistance to buying into the current, totally pathologized view of Alzheimer's. I wanted to greet its course with my mind as open as possible. I didn't want to live in fear. I wanted to be open and curious, unencumbered by other people's models.

I often thought back to an exchange with my beloved friend Blanche, who in her elder years gradually lost her sight to glaucoma. When I went to visit her for her ninetieth birthday, I asked her what it was like for her now that she was totally blind.

She tipped her delicate head to one side, thought for a moment, and said in her gentle but authoritative voice, "I treat everything as new experience. That seems to be the secret to handling my blindness."

"Treat everything as new experience."

What a wonderful attitude with which to meet life! It means experiencing life without all the mental baggage that most of us carry around—the array of opinions, preconceptions, and fixed views that become the lens through which we see our lives. Her words echoed the famous phrase "beginner's mind," the words of Suzuki Roshi's classic book *Zen Mind, Beginner's Mind*.

Any disease, or indeed any process of loss, invites us to greet it as new experience, and this perspective helped me to keep reactivity and judgment out of charged situations. I'm sure Hob's playful and somewhat contrary nature contributed to how I approached his situation. While he was disarmingly open, often startling people with the ease with which he spoke about having the disease, he periodically talked with me about his disbelief about the diagnosis. He said many times, "I'm going to beat this. I may be the first person to do it, but that's how I'm looking at it."

Or another time much later, when intelligible statements

were few and far between, he said emphatically:

"They call it Alzheimer's, but I don't call it anything!"

Denial is well known in medical circles as one of the forms of coping with life-threatening illness. If it was working for Hob, so much the better. Other levels of acceptance might come in their own time.

⸺ ⸺ ❧ ⸺ ⸺

One of the most critical times for Hob was the time between sleep and waking, especially after his afternoon naps. I remembered one day when he had greeted me almost frantically. He began to describe what he was experiencing, speaking quickly but with lapses between his phrases. He fired off his words as if talking would help to reassemble the scattered pieces of his inner world.

"When I woke up a few minutes ago, I didn't know where I was . . . where anybody was . . . where you were. . . . I didn't know who I was. . . . I've dropped out of everybody else's time . . . . I could have been asleep two hundred years. . . . I can't imagine everybody else's time when I'm disoriented like this. . . ."

Amidst tears, his and mine, I tried to help him put the pieces back together. Even with his discontinuous sentences, I was struck by how aware he was of what was going on.

"Don't take anything I'm saying too seriously," he said toward the end of our conversation. Not an easy request.

"I just wish I could eliminate all this. Turn it around," he added.

Amazingly, the truth was that even with all the signs—this relentless process of deterioration—some part of me still clung to the sense that under the confusion he was still well, that somehow he might even bounce back. My mind automatically bargained: maybe this was just a temporary state of affairs. He seemed so healthy in every other way. How challenging to accept that this process was final, headed inexorably toward loss of mind, loss of communication, eventually death. Much to ponder. Much to open to. Much to accept.

He described his experience that afternoon as "having the blackboard totally wiped clean." No thoughts arising. No recognition of anything. Total blankness. Nothing. What was that like for him? Were these states at all similar to the moments between thoughts that occur during meditation? In meditation, awareness is still present. I could see that his awareness was still intact but couldn't help wondering how long it would last.

——— ⬡ ———

Sometimes the whole equation turned over. Instead of the treacherous, post-nap landscapes of his mind, Hob would awake on some mornings in what he described as "a beatific state." On those mornings—and it happened on and off for months—he lingered in bed, entirely peaceful, a slight smile softening the lines in his face. He looked ageless, childlike.

"Inwardly, I have a wonderful view of things," he once said, attempting to convey what it was like.

"All that's in there seems organized, clear, as if the innate order of the universe is all there, in my head. There aren't any words. It's beautiful. A state of grace. I wish I could stay there, but of course," and he chuckled as he finished the sentence, "that's not the way it is."

Whenever those early morning states of grace occurred, he moved into the day with another level of gentleness and ease. His state was contagious. I felt something unnamable which affected my day as well, another one of the hidden gifts in this strange, unpredictable journey.

Then, before I realized it, we were back with the post-nap roller coaster. During a particularly disorienting conversation, it was clear that Hob wasn't recognizing my references to familiar places in our neighborhood. At first I couldn't believe that he was so confused. Again, my mind resisted and bargained. Was he pretending? Playing games with me? My mind, so conditioned to the way things had been, balked at these assaults on its reasonable ways! Stop kidding me! Disbelief and shock were now constant companions.

Incredulous as I was, I gathered myself to be as fully present as I could. I was expectant with no expectations. My awareness sharpened; I was awake to the moment, to each breath, to all the nuances of his expression and his struggle for words. Sometimes I was split between two realities. In one I conversed with him, trying to maintain equanimity and absolute non-judgment. In the other I was stunned beyond feeling, groping my way—

sentence by sentence—to a place where we could meet and stand safely together. But we were on shifting ground.

I treated his confused phrases like koans; they echoed in my mind. His words were signals from his inner world trying to connect with mine, out of the confusion of his strange mind-states.

Later in the day, he confessed to me, "When you came in after my nap, I didn't recognize you. Not right away. But I don't want you to worry. It wasn't for long."

Had I heard him correctly? Could I let his words in?

"That must be distressing. Really unsettling," I replied, aware of the effort it took to let the truth penetrate.

"Yes, it passed pretty quickly," he continued, "but it's an indication of things to come. That's what happened to your mother. Not recognizing people. But don't worry. This was just a flash. The other is still a long way off."

Was it? That's the wonder of this disease — its unpredictability.

⁂

With the familiar expression that appeared when Hob was about to say something witty, another day he announced with great solemnity: "The mind has no fences. And no defenses."

I broke out laughing, a welcome release after a long period of trying to decode his language. Confusion was riding high, especially around time and place. In anticipation of an upcoming trip, he was already working the idea of Seattle, our destination, into his inner world. But where were the lines now between inner and outer? I would recognize his far-away look and then the moment of intense focus, as though he were reaching for some thread that might lead him back through the labyrinth of disconnected images to a lost reality.

I was humbled by how much psychic energy it took for me to decipher his mental states. I ricocheted between feelings of great tenderness and wild frustration. I could track my vacillations but I couldn't always modulate them. I could feel how my usual resilience became strained. I felt like a lonely pilgrim, urgently seeking my way through perilous, mountainous territory. Suddenly I found myself hanging on to a fraying, swinging rope, pulling myself, hand over hand, across a cavernous abyss. This was my current image of survival.

⸻ ❦ ⸻

Then along would come one of my dreams to elucidate the challenges in symbolic language. They were a reality check for me that I had come to trust. During Hob's illness, some of the dreams were as vivid as waking life—sometimes more so—because such is the power of symbol to reverberate in our consciousness in a timeless way.

I am helping to teach children who are disabled in some way, like a children's version of Alzheimer's. The children have left for the day, and as I turn toward the left, I see that there is an unusual beach. It isn't made of sand but of very small, smooth stones. Scattered all through the stones are exquisitely beautiful shells with different markings. I see a white shell that has unusual, elaborate red patterns on it. I pick it up and hold it in my hand, marveling at the intricacy of the patterns and amazed at the treasure that I've found.

Meanwhile, the person who runs this place is handing out something to the other people who are working with us. They are pieces of yellowed antique paper, relics from an old map of South Asia. As she holds the last relic of the map in her hand, I assume it is for me. But it isn't; it's for her. I feel disheartened. I've missed out on getting my piece of the map.

The dream presented its message with ruthless clarity. I often shared dreams with Hob, but these days I hesitated to share strong feelings because they upset him. At breakfast that morning, he began talking about his difficulties with the Boston Alzheimer's Center where he had started to go one day a week. So the topic of difficulties was already on the table.

I began to recount the dream. As I did, my tears surprised me. Even with the beautiful shell, the dominant image was that I'd lost the map. The dream, as I recounted it, was charged with feeling. Indeed, the last few days had been difficult. I felt "worn to a basting thread," as my mother used to call this state, trying so hard to make everything work. Obviously it took great effort to help Hob stay afloat, so it was hardly any wonder that I sometimes plummeted myself.

Even though I knew that my emotional intensity was distressing to him, it was not right to hide my grief all the time, either. I realized that sometimes we needed to grieve together;

our shared tears were a relief. *Ah . . . passing show . . . hang on!*
I told myself.

Like the gift of the shell in the dream, the phrase "passing
show" had surfaced at that moment, a bit of practical wisdom
from one of my meditation teachers who used it as a way to
greet the tough stuff in life. After all, he'd say, everything in life
is shifting, changing and impermanent. "Passing show" became
a reassuring phrase for me, like a mantra which I'd call up in difficult moments. It softened the grievous image of the lost map.

The Challenges of Mental Loss
Reflections

* There are ways to lighten, even transform, the burdens of suffering by reflecting on what we can learn
from difficult circumstances. Are you being invited
to develop a certain quality? Or being reminded that
you're not in this alone, that how you handle any illness can be helpful or inspiring for others? As you go
along, you may find that people turn to you for help
when they have to deal with Alzheimer's. And then all
you have learned will be a gift for others.

* Whether or not it arises overtly, the subject of death
takes all of us to the deepest places of love and pain. We
can listen for any hints of whether it's on the patient's
mind. Do they question whether life is worth it any-

more, or give signs that they want to give up, or end their suffering? It's important to listen unconditionally and affirm that these feelings are natural for anyone in their situation.

In our case, the subject of death was one we dealt with openly. At one point, it made the world of difference to ask friends to help us discuss the enormity of the subject. All of us need to remember that every issue we face, no matter how harrowing or appalling, has been experienced before. Asking for help from family, friend, or professional is always worth considering.

* It's the nature of this disease that we must make the shift from a world woven out of words to a world unraveling into confusion and silence. This is a heart-rending challenge. To begin by recognizing this will make us more compassionate toward the patient and ourselves, especially when frustration, exasperation, and anger flare.

Loss is an inevitable part of later life—every one of us confronts it sooner or later. In our case, a friend invited Hob to change his perspective, to reframe how he responded to his loss of words and his fear of dependence. "Consider it a spiritual discipline and be open to receiving from others," the friend said. That's a tall order and a radical statement, but it helped!

Suggestions

* If you can find ways to shift moments of loss and confusion toward something lighter, it helps. As with a child, you can divert the patient's attention with distraction, touch, singing, a new activity, and so on. You can also hang in there with him and try together to find his meanings, but this may also lead to further frustration. These are delicate choice points.

* Do everything you can to stay in touch with the positive aspects of your relationship: the warm memories you share, the special everyday moments, the simple comfort of touch. All the heartbreaks of this illness can begin to overshadow your relationship so that, unconsciously, you end up relating more to the disease than to the one who has it. Although everything becomes increasingly difficult in the advanced stages, still we need to remember that some fragment of consciousness remains. Just being present, caring, reassuring, appreciative, touching—all these little gestures matter, regardless of how confused or vacant the patient's mind appears to be.

* Since those with Alzheimer's are living a life of constant losses, it's important to find even the smallest ways to reassure them and name how they are doing well. For example: "It's so great that you can help me set the table" (even if they get confused), "I love to see you smile" (even though smiles may gradually disappear), or "Thanks for asking me to come and sit with you."

You can also recall for them positive times from their past when they did something creative, surprising, funny, memorable, or kind. Remember that they are losing memories, and you can become the guardian of the treasures of their past. It's wonderful to invoke pleasant moments for them. Reminiscing over old photographs or looking at pictures in a magazine or book can have a similar effect.

If your relationship with the patient is difficult, remember that Alzheimer's has a way of erasing (and yes, sometimes amplifying) troublesome qualities. Be open to the possibility of unexpected positive shifts in the relationship that, paradoxically, are brought about by what the illness takes away. For example, someone who was hypercritical, imperious, and cold may become increasingly accepting, gentle, and loving.

Seed Thoughts

Let me be creative in handling the difficult situations.

I will affirm the positive aspects of our relationship.

Let me reframe some of the challenges.

CHAPTER SIX

FROM COPPER TO GOLD

"I think I'm headed for the observer's role," declared Hob one morning, using one of his occasional pronouncements that heralded a new phase in the order of things. It had been four years since that May morning at the diagnostic clinic. The losses had come silently, out of nowhere. For example, his inability to turn on the radio in spite of the signs that we placed on it and our other appliances. Such simple things we do all day long without giving them any thought. "I'm always being tricked by things!" he said that day, chuckling to himself. "I wish I could send away for a gathered self and have it delivered COD!"

Sometimes my initial response was irritation. His need for help invariably came when I was immersed in my own activity. Besides continuing to teach and write, my life at home seemed increasingly carved into pieces—a mosaic of responding, helping, changing directions, accepting interruptions.

On the subject of interruptions, which become the warp and woof of the caregiver's life, I would remember messages from my past that served me in handling them. I recalled a small exchange that had happened in Switzerland the day we arrived for a two-week retreat with Hugo, a teacher in the tradition of Ramana Maharshi, a much-loved twentieth-century Indian saint. We had traveled to a spectacular valley where streams poured down the mountainside and the sound of falling water accompanied us everywhere. In early July, the fields were still blanketed with wildflowers and the cows pastured there wore wide leather collars from which hung large cowbells that sounded gently as they grazed. We had climbed the hill up to Hugo's house, where we found him outside the kitchen door, piling wood for the stove.

"Hello. Sorry—it looks like we're interrupting you," I said, one of those automatic pleasantries upon meeting someone for the first time.

He looked up, smiled, and answered quietly:

"There are no interruptions."

Hugo's words struck me. As someone who can find interruptions a test of patience, I often reflected on that statement. In caretaking someone with dementia, it's a valuable mantra. By this time in Hob's illness, he needed my assistance with an increasing number of things—retrieve a word, turn something on, find some object—an endless array of little demands. At times, in response to all his needs, I felt that my sense of self was slowly fragmenting. The challenge was clear enough: how to live each day as a seamless web of events, one flowing into the other with ease and flexibility. It was most important now because each day was shot through with the unexpected.

As with the interruptions, I began to watch for other patterns in the caregiving process. Thanks to the ongoing help of Diane who companioned Hob part of four days a week, I continued to lead my own life separate from his. For three years we had been blessed by the steady, playful presence of Diane, whose arrival in the morning made me feel as if the sun had just come out. She was lighthearted by nature, with a playful sense of humor that embroidered almost every situation. When she first came, Hob thought she was there to help me, an ideal arrangement since our goal was to support his sense of independence. Over the three years, she moved into the role of companion so inconspicuously that he hardly seemed to notice. She both adored and respected him, laughing delightedly at his antics with words. Humor and lightness must be two of the most valuable qualities in a caregiver, and she had both in abundance.

Even with her invaluable help, however, caregiving was still the primary thread that wove through my life. As such, I was determined to understand the intricacies that were involved. I studied all the permutations of caregiving as if my life depended on it, because in some ways it did. From my years as a therapist I knew the perils of burnout, a danger in being the person who spent the most time with him.

I also felt the impact of our age difference. He was seventy-six in the fourth year since the diagnosis; I was only sixty-two. We were in different stages of the life cycle. His life was winding down. I was vibrant and fully engaged in a life that seemed to extend into the distant future. Had I not felt that destiny had handed us this journey to do together, I might have resented being thrust into the caregiving role at a relatively young age. Certainly there were times when I felt burdened, but the depth of our journey together, over thirty-five years, far outweighed those feelings; it fired my commitment and sustained me.

I surprised even myself by my determination to make his last years as smooth and happy as possible. I was his fierce protector and his advocate in everything to do with his health care, by then a series of various appointments. In addition, I sought out alternative therapies for him, like acupuncture, massage, and the naturopathic doctor who put him on an elaborate regimen of supplements, special foods, and tinctures all intended to support brain function. Although we couldn't prove it scientifically, Hob and I felt, as did our family, that the naturopathic program contributed to his having more quality time. He especially welcomed his weekly session of massage therapy. The physicality and loving care of the massage was comforting. Afterward he seemed more present and mentally aware.

To continue Hob's lifelong commitment to exercise, important for anyone with Alzheimer's, we found Sean, a young artist who took him swimming several times a week. Sean's easy and gentle ways captured Hob's affection, so these swimming expeditions were high points in the week. And Simon, who came to play guitar, patiently played and replayed the few pieces Hob could still remember. I was also Hob's social director, inviting friends to visit, to sing, to take him for walks. I used to joke with him that sometimes I felt like I was organizing the invasion of Normandy—so much to be handled, arranged, juggled, explained—to maintain his quality of life. *What a trip!* I'd say to myself in wonder and sometimes in overwhelm.

It is difficult to convey to the uninitiated what this form of caregiving was like. It became my primary focus. Maybe that was due to my nature, but I'm convinced that almost every Alzheimer's caregiver will nod their head and say, "Yes, that was true for me, too." Anything else that was part of my life then—teaching, writing, friendship, family, retreats, household-ing—was eclipsed. It all took extraordinary psychic energy.

I recognized the parallels to caring for a young child. My awareness had to be turned outward where I was both cen-tered in my own activity yet simultaneously attuned to him. I needed to be aware of where he was, what he was doing—or not doing.

In conversation I also needed to be attuned in a special way. I listened for meanings, offered the lost word, guessed at the irre-trievable name, tried to find the threads of connection between topics. Sometimes it felt as if we were playing a complicated guessing game, like charades or twenty questions, only far more convoluted than either. Often Hob just started talking about something as if I'd know—of course!—exactly what was on his mind. Until I figured out what he was talking about, I was in free fall, between knowing and not knowing. I was attentive in those moments, my mind still, thought suspended. Difficult as these times were, they were also like gifts. When we have "don't know mind," as our first Zen teacher called it, we live with the gift of immediacy. There was only that priceless moment where Hob and I, deeply bonded by our shared lives, sought to meet in unfamiliar dimensions of reality.

The episodes that confronted us with our helplessness came like thunder in the night. It was after dinner. Hob had fallen asleep again on the love seat next to the planting window. I had tried to read aloud with him, but he kept drifting off.

"Hobbie, time to wake up. Time for us to go to bed."

"It is going to be all right."

"Yes, it is going to be all right. And it's time for us to go to bed."

"It's going to be all right," he repeated.

I reached for his hands to help him stand, but he resisted, pulling me down beside him.

"It's going to be all right," he kept saying insistently, as though I had failed to get something important.

This sequence of exchanges continued for several tedious rounds—my trying to get him to stand, his resisting.

I realized my strategy wasn't working. Once again, different agendas, different rhythms. I laid my head against his cheek and began to hum the South African freedom song he loved.

"Tumamena, Tumamena." I felt something shift slightly within him, and he started to hum very quietly, off tune. Uncharacteristic for him. He had a fine ear for music and a beautiful singing voice. We sang several verses, but I could feel

how he was locked into some inaccessible mind-state. I knew I had to keep singing. Maybe that would be the key to our deadlocked situation. Very quietly, I started to sing one of his favorite chants. He attempted to come in with the second part, but faltered and murmured, humming, a different melody along side of mine.

Silence. He was obviously still in another realm of consciousness. I felt the tiniest thread of connection between us.

I stood up again and took his hands. He stood up.

"Come, let's go upstairs."

"Why are you doing this?"

He pulled against me, aggressively. He looked at me intensely, a slightly hostile, testing expression, as if he were possessed by some inexplicable force.

"What's happening? What are you feeling?" I asked.

"It's going to be all right."

"Yes, it will," I reassured him, "but will you come with me?"

"Why?"

He began to back up toward the couch. We were trapped in a cul-de-sac of miscommunication, neither of us able get through to the other.

I steadied myself, centered myself in my breath. Each moment felt timeless, attenuated by the intensity of the situation. But I couldn't keep away the unsettling thought: what if I couldn't get him to go anywhere? Let him sleep on the couch? Was this the end of our being able to communicate or just another episode of disconnection? Who would I call for help?

"What's happened here?" he asked, breaking into my thoughts.

"Does the room seem strange? Is there something that troubles you between here and the stairs?"

He looked at me curiously. "Yes. What are you doing?"

"We're going upstairs. Here, let me lead you. All you have to do is keep hold of my hand."

I cajoled him along, step by step. The stairs must have seemed imposing. He stopped. I coaxed, seeking to find just the right pressure of encouragement and support, without letting impatience or coercion enter.

"It's going to be all right."

"Yes, it is. We're almost there."

As we came into the bedroom, it felt like a victory. We'd been in this strange world of disconnection for almost half an hour. I undressed him and handed him his toothbrush. He looked at it and asked, "What's this for?" But as soon as I put it in his mouth and began brushing, he reached up and continued to brush. As I tucked him into bed and laid my cheek against his, it all felt so reminiscent of caring for a child. What was he experiencing? Was he really all right, as he'd kept repeating? I looked at his closed eyes and mane of silver hair, his face softened in a peaceful expression.

Suddenly, everything expanded for me into a moment of timelessness. What a mystery life is! What is it that had brought us together—this love, our struggles and joys, failures and triumphs, the beauty of this moment?

No answers for the ultimate questions. "Don't know mind" again. I undressed and eased into bed beside him. As I had many times before, I realized these could be our last moments together—lying together, cheek against cheek. I felt a flood of tenderness, of love. He could die anytime now. Tonight even. How much we assume.

"Are you okay?" I asked.

"*Hmmmm* . . . Thank you."

"Sleep well. . . . I love you. . . . I love you." No response.

"Did you take that in?"

"Yes, thank you, thank you."

Whatever the state of his mind, some connection was back, frail and tender.

Into the midst of the most challenging times, the dreams would come, messengers from another realm. They reassured me that at some level all was well. I marveled at the capacity of the unconscious to provide images that offered balance and inspiration. The dreams were a form of grace.

I am standing on a dock at the edge of a bay, where the water is so clear and pure that I can see far beneath the surface. As I stand looking into the water, I see a dark shape swimming around in all directions, very fast, very playfully, and realize it is a dolphin. I remember that a guide in Florida had told us that dolphins love playfulness and noise, so I walk to the very edge of the dock, gather all of my energy, and make an amazing, first-time-ever sound—very high, almost out of human hearing—a powerful sound that startles even me. The dolphin immediately changes course and swims very fast toward me, leaps out of the water, and lands in my lap. It settles down, contentedly, to stay. Once out of the water, it looks a little more like a seal or a large version of a kid's toy animal, but still it is definitely a dolphin.

I awoke from the dream feeling washed in happiness. As one does upon waking from a big dream, I lay still, trying to stay close to dream consciousness. I needed this ally from the ocean's depths, this responsive, playful creature who thrilled me by landing in my lap.

Other dolphin images began to emerge. Many years earlier, Hob and I had gone to Florida to swim with the dolphins at a place where they were used for healing. Autistic children, disturbed teenagers, people with life-threatening illness, and ordinary people like us came to experience being in their presence. While the staff helped the autistic children relate to the dolphins in a nearby pool, we swam in the large, deep tanks that were temporary home to two dolphins.

We had a friend with cancer who had gone there with the hope that contact with the dolphins would help him heal. He described how one of them swam close beside him for an extended time. As he gazed into the dolphin's eye, he had an extraordinary experience. Man and dolphin, moving slowly, effortlessly through water, contemplating one another, their gaze holding. He slipped into an altered state and beheld the universe in the depths of the dolphin's eye, sensing a preternatural wisdom streaming toward him.

Our friend described the experience as a defining moment in his life, a moment in which everything was in divine order. He attributed his healing from cancer to a combination of elements which climaxed in his encounter with the dolphin.

I had heard other amazing stories about interactions between humans and dolphins, such as the experiments to understand their language, and especially the reports of how dolphins had rescued people who were drowning. The prospect of swimming with them was thrilling, also daunting. The tanks were large and deep. Equipped with goggles and flippers, I jumped in. They swam like lightning. I'd catch a glimpse of a great grey body flying past me. Then gone. Only fleeting glimpses, as the two dolphins played tag with each other. They appeared to ignore the three humans who were frantically swimming around in their watery world.

For half an hour I set new swimming records for myself. I alternated between great surging strokes, then slowed down, or dove deep, or flipped around—trying to maintain contact. They played in my peripheral vision, then streaked by or paused momentarily, then gone again.

Finally, totally winded, I treaded water at the far side of the tank and decided to wait. Moments later I glimpsed a dolphin off to my right. It gentled its pace and allowed me to reposition myself along its side. Eye to eye, we swam along slowly. I reached out and stroked the side of its smooth body. It was thrilling to be swimming so close to this elegant creature with its generous smile. What was passing between us? I felt we were in some kind of communication—a sense of connection, gratitude and appreciation. Awe and wonder.

My experience with the dolphins had come during a crisis period in my life, a dark night of the soul. I was healing from the pain of spiritual disillusionment. I had sought healing in several forms—therapy, bodywork, and energy healing. Then I swam with the dolphins. Afterward, I realized how my encounter with them had wrought some shift in my psyche. Several indigenous and shamanic traditions speak about the power of having allies in the natural world. Through dreams, visions, or intuition, those who are part of these traditions feel a special connection with certain animals, birds, or other creatures. Similarly, I now felt a special relationship with dolphins. They had become my symbol of gentleness, healing, and freedom. That same year, still long before Hob's illness appeared, I had started to paint again. I did a series of large, semi-abstract acrylics, using art to express the intense range of feelings that were part of that dark period. After swimming with the dolphins, they appeared in one painting after another. Dynamic and free, they swam across the paper in great sweeping arcs, leapt out of waves of color and line, dove into spiraling light. Dolphin energy had released a new form of expressiveness in my art.

They also appeared as images of healing in my dreams, a series of dreams in which dolphins appeared. And here once again, many years later during a difficult period of care-taking, a dolphin had appeared as an ally in a dream, which inspired me for a long time afterward.

—✦— ✦ —✦—

It was the middle of the night. I awoke slowly, aware that Hob had moved closer to me with an unfamiliar urgency.

"I don't know what's wrong with me. I haven't been asleep at all. I'm afraid. I'm feeling a lot of fear. I think I'm bottoming out. Where is it that we're supposed to be going? What am I supposed to be doing? I'm really confused. I understand only about ten percent of what's going on now. My mind is really going and it scares me."

I began to reassure him, reminding him that I was with him and that I would stand by him no matter what happened. My reassurances sounded feeble in the face of his fear. Still wrapped in the heaviness of sleep, I added, "Maybe we should get Jim and Louise over again so we can talk about these worries. Have them witness where we are now."

"What are you talking about? I don't know what they have to do with this."

I felt the familiar pang of loss as I realized he didn't remember our meeting from the previous fall. Why should he? This was about memory loss. As I lay next to him in the darkened room, I felt my helplessness and our vulnerability.

"Listen," I replied. "Let's let all this wait until morning, until the brightness of day. It all looms much larger in the night. We'll talk about it in the morning. It's going to be all right," I said, invoking the words he had used during difficult moments. He moved closer. I could feel his fear in how he reached for me.

Was this the beginning of a new phase? Or was he disoriented by his fear, lack of sleep, and the darkness? I reminded myself that the disease appeared in countless guises, that life around Hob was not always as it appeared, and that it changed unpredictably many times each day. Yet his fear was palpable. It was the strongest statement about his disease that he'd spoken in many months.

⁕ ⁕ ⁕

It was New Year's Day, traditionally a day of new beginnings, of resolutions and intention. The sky was clear, the day blustery and very cold. Having set aside some quiet time for reflection, I picked up a favorite book with the intention of opening it randomly to see what message for the day might be there. The book was a collection of writings by Rumi, the fourteenth-century Sufi mystic and poet. As I opened the deep red covers with their graceful Persian designs, I prayed for inspiration. My eye fell two-thirds of the way down the right-hand page, and these were the words that greeted me.

> **Always check your inner state**
> **with the lord of your heart.**
> **Copper doesn't know it's copper,**
> **until it's changed to gold.**
> **Your loving doesn't know its majesty,**
> **until it knows its helplessness.**[1]

What a startling message to leap off the page at me! I read and reread the words, and finally copied them onto a note card that was to live on my desk altar for many months.

There is no explanation for the moments of mystery when the universe provides messages of reassurance and connection. In spite of all the challenges, the message said all is well at the deepest level, where we can find meaning, even transformation, in the midst of what is most difficult. The image of transformation—of copper into gold—comes from alchemy, the medieval tradition that experimented with how to transmute base metal into gold. It is a metaphor for the soul's journey from the limited, self-oriented ego to the freedom of the liberated Self, the purpose of all spiritual practices.

"Always check your inner state with the lord of your heart." That first line was inspiring, reminiscent of the loving attention of mindfulness, or in Christian parlance, the practice of the presence of God. The words pointed to a great and often hidden mystery: that in accepting our helplessness, we discover the deepest sources of our loving. That's possible for everyone around a loved one with serious illness: spouse, family members, friends. The love would carry us through. Rumi's words would accompany me through what lay ahead.

<hr>

What lay ahead were the endless challenges of being so close to a loved one whose mind was going. Hob swung wildly between clarity and confusion. His sense of reality shifted, dissolved, and reformed with vertiginous regularity. His mental states were affecting me.

At unpredictable times, for example, I'd find myself searching for words. I'd forget what I was about to do. Sometimes my mind drifting aimlessly, befogged and disengaged. We joked about the contagious aspect of Alzheimer's, but it was unsettling.

The strains of caregiving were subterranean, sometimes invisible even to me. I knew from the years of my mother's decline that grief often masks as fatigue. It's the heavy, down-pulling feeling of unshed tears. Then some little incident would come along, like Hob struggling to tie his shoelaces. My heart would break for him. Suddenly tears overflowed. But I had to walk away to hide them, for now, with his acute sensitivity, my distress became his distress.

The stresses of caregiving surfaced in wild dreams where I would find myself threatened by flooded rivers, towering waves, or high, precipitous landscapes. In the middle of the night, I would wake up to my own cries of alarm and lie in the dark with a pounding heart.

"You've changed," Hob said to me one day. "You order me around all the time and get that edge on your voice."

His words entered like an arrow. He was amazingly perceptive; I well knew when I slipped from gentle guide to irritated general. At times I felt bored and frustrated, sick to death of the whole situation. I wondered when and how it would ever end. Then I felt shame for such thoughts, followed by a surge of love for this person with whom I'd shared a life. Emotional yo-yo—that's the way it was sometimes.

In the midst of the loss and increasing confusion, Hob's flashes of wisdom still shone through. We got deeply entangled one morning when he'd come in before dawn to where I was sleeping, now often in another room because his nights were restless. Angry at being awakened, I grudgingly went back to our bed but lay there, hot with resentment, uselessly trying to sleep again.

As we were getting up, he said in a firm and caring way, "Don't sacrifice yourself for me."

He knew. That's exactly what I'd done. Sacrifice breeds resentment. How to balance my life while living with someone whose life was careening out of balance? Of course it was all about perspective—easy to talk about, hard to remember.

That summer, the fifth since Hob's diagnosis, I was having tea with a friend, a nun in the Tibetan tradition. She was a Westerner, and so we could commiserate over the gap between the ideals of Buddhist teachings and the realities of caring for someone with dementia. Hob and I, we decided, were taking a crash course in impermanence. The law of impermanence, one of the most pivotal of the Buddha's teachings, was only an idea, an intellectual toy, until one lived with life-threatening illness.

"All these difficulties that he's starting to have—like agitation, paranoia, fear—they won't be there at death," she pointed out, "because death will be liberation from the body, the mind, and the disease. This is just a passing phase, a chapter in his lifetime," she said lightly.

"My teacher used to say that this lifetime is like sitting

down in a chair for a short while, then getting up and moving on to the next life," she continued. "I used to think that was a very whimsical perspective on the very complex subject of reincarnation!"

I told her about how hard it was to keep my balance with the demands of caregiving.

"Maybe you're already aware of this," she replied, "but in Buddhism we talk about the principle of the two benefits. The idea is very simple. For anything to be of benefit to another person, it must also be balanced with benefit to oneself. We can all get trapped into giving too much of ourselves and lose the balance in relationships. That's where this idea of the two benefits can be a helpful reminder."

And that's what it became for me. This principle has its own echoes in Western psychology with theories of codependence, but hearing an unexpected phrase—that of the two benefits— from another tradition gave me a new perspective on a critical issue. To give too much is draining; it causes resentment and anger. If we give and give, we drain our reservoir of energy, until we become not the one sacrificing but the sacrificed.

My family of origin had a derisive expression for this pattern. "You're being an E.C.M.," a sibling would declare when one of us had fallen into self-righteous sacrifice. The acronym stood for "Early Christian Martyr." The phrase was curiously satisfying and corrective.

Interestingly, the word *sacrifice*, familiar to the Christian tradition, doesn't occur in Buddhist parlance. Rather, Buddhism speaks of wisdom and compassion as being like the wings of a bird. One without the other, and the bird cannot fly. Wisdom without compassion is unsupported by wise action; compassion without wisdom can become idiot compassion, as one Buddhist teacher called it. And so the principle of the two benefits proved to be another valuable coping tool.

"I need you to keep me afloat," declared Hob as I entered the bedroom. He was sitting on the edge of the bed, head in his hands, his body bent over in a disconsolate posture.

"What's happening? You seem so tired."

"I feel as though depression is right around the corner, waiting to take over," he replied, heaviness weighing on every word.

"This is so hard—the hardest thing you've ever had to do. *We've* ever had to do," I replied. "You know, I keep trying to feel what this must be like for you. I imagine that it's like being suspended in space with nothing to hold on to."

"Yes, that's right. That's what it's like. I try to get hold of something, but there's nothing. No handholds. Nothing."

I paused, gathering my inner strength, struggling to reconnect with the conviction that had sustained me for the last five years.

"Remember? We said at the beginning, when you got the diagnosis, that this is our journey, that at some level our souls must have chosen to do this one together. It helps me to remember that. Not to deny how hard it is or anything, but just to remember the bigger perspective."

"I know," he replied, "but I'm really losing it. How can I have anything to do with the class at the Center? Feels like everything is unraveling. I can't teach anything anymore."

Every Thursday Hob had been going to the Boston Alzheimer's Center, which had an excellent day program for people with dementia. At first he resisted going; he asserted that he wasn't in the same place as most of the people who attended, which at the beginning was true. But I needed the respite. Besides, I reasoned, it would offer him a feeling of community as well as varied activities.

The staff members were wonderful about encouraging the participants to share whatever they could—playing guitar, singing, reading poetry, gardening, and other hobbies. Assuring Hob of their support, the staff encouraged him to offer a meditation class as a way to honor what he'd been doing for years. When he began the class he could only offer fragments of what he once knew, but a staff member who also knew something about meditation assisted him as needed.

Each Wednesday before the class, Hob and I would figure out what to focus on that week. I had to take the lead with this weekly project because he would never have remembered the class, much less been able to initiate such a complicated task. I would find a statement, quotation, or simple guided meditation. We'd discuss the various possibilities. I would sense which option appealed to him, to make the final choice. This was a challenge. He could no longer make choices, but I wanted to give him the feeling that he'd participated, even if it involved more negotiating, coaxing, time. Now, as he sat on the bed in the throes of a sinking spell, he anguished over the realization of how little he could bring to the class—his last class.

"Feeling as if your teaching's over, that's a really hard one," I said, scarcely able to find words to honor the loss he must be feeling.

"But you know what we've got to remember?" I continued. "It's *how* you live this journey. It's no longer about words and sutras and Buddhist philosophy; it's about how you're living now. I think you forget how amazingly you're doing. Your humor, your acceptance, your lightness of spirit. That's what's inspiring. That's the way you're teaching now."

He was sitting up now, listening. This little miracle had happened again. When we reflected on the spacious possibilities of our situation, it became more manageable. These shifts were grace, copper turning into gold. The gift came when both of us reconnected with the deeper purpose. Then we carried the burdens and the opportunities together. Everything seemed possible once again.

As we stood up, he turned to look at me. His eyes were brimming with tears.

"Thank you for being so many people."

⸎ ⸎ ⸎

I woke up one day to the realization of another change in Hob.

He was quieter now, especially when friends were around.

"It's getting harder to talk," he said to me one day. "I feel as if I have to drop out of conversation because I can't remember where it started. I can't catch it, as though everything is vague and very far away."

What was it like for him to feel his ability to communicate slowly cut off? How did he tolerate the loneliness of his dissolving world? Did he notice during conversations how people often no longer looked at him, as if he had ceased to exist? Although this is a common reflex around someone with dementia, it's painful to watch. Unconsciously, people cut him out of conversation—visually—as if he weren't there. In a group of people, our eyes tend to go toward the person who is talking, where the energy is. The quiet one seems to disappear from the circle.

No wonder Hob had begun to speak again about death. Sometimes he made simple, matter-of-fact remarks.

"Now I'm nearing the finish line of life."

Or, with his wry sense of humor, "Get me out of this life! Everything's dissolving. Time to let go of this incarnation!"

Other times, he recited poetry. He continued to access his vast repository of random quotes and poems. One day, when I asked him how he had memorized so much poetry, he replied that he hadn't really tried; the lines stuck like burrs, inscribing themselves in his memory. All he needed was an association and the lines poured forth. He spoke with force and delight:

> **Oh as I was young and easy in the mercy of his means,**
> **Time held me green and dying**
> **Though I sang in my chains like the sea.**

At my request, Hob repeated the lines with pleasure. I found out later that they were an excerpt from "Fern Hill" by Dylan Thomas.[2]

That evening as he headed for his favorite chair in the family room, he announced seemingly out of nowhere:

"I'll let you know when death arrives. It's much easier than people think."

I believed him.

THE MANY GUISES OF CAREGIVING
Reflections

* As caregivers, we constantly are thinking our way into an Alzheimer's reality. What is she thinking or feeling? What is he trying to say? Where is her mind? What new losses am I witnessing? This takes a lot of psychic energy and can be wearing, tedious, and emotionally exhausting. It helped me to acknowledge that being a caregiver to someone with dementia was the hardest thing I'd ever done in my life. And furthermore, the strains and stresses are largely invisible to those around us.

* Caregiving involves an endless array of roles. We become the patient's advocate, social director, protector, comforter, ally, initiator, driver, cook, secretary, financial manager, entertainer, word finder, prompter, memory jogger—to name a few. We become

the mind for the one who is losing it—a monumental task!

If you consider the mythic dimensions of this illness, this is surely your version of the hero's journey. It tests those who are touched by it, and all great tests are a form of initiation. This is another example of shifting your perspective toward the situation.

* Caregiving makes endless demands on us. Therefore, it's valuable to stay in touch with what I've called the meta perspectives. For example, this is the final chapter of your relationship. It involves a combination of challenges and opportunities more amplified than ever before. The question is whether you recognize them and how you want to respond.

* As this is a disease of loss, it may seem impossible to find anything redeeming in the face of such pain. Yet we can find meaning in hidden places—"the grace of diminishment"—as Teilhard de Chardin put it. Some possible examples: the prospect of death invites us to treasure the ordinary moments; our poignant feelings and shared vulnerabilities can lead to more tenderness between us; we can appreciate the few capacities our loved one still has—to hum a song, sit in the garden, hold a grandchild, watch a movie. Something as seemingly ordinary as touch takes on heightened tenderness; the reciprocal squeeze of a hand affirms that you

are still in touch, even if all the words are gone.

* When I first read the quotation that inspired the title of this book, the words hit me with the force of revelation. "Your loving doesn't know its majesty until it knows its helplessness," Rumi wrote. Some people may think that is a depressing statement, but upon reflection it becomes arresting and inspiring. It acknowledges the fact—especially true in old age—that we become increasingly helpless. Fighting that reality causes suffering; acceptance of it frees us.

Although seemingly paradoxical, when we accept that we are helpless to change the realities of living with dementia—or loss of any kind—we may gradually discover the deepest sources of our loving. For love enables us to handle the greatest challenges that life presents.

Suggestions

* The caregiver's life increasingly fills with demands and interruptions. It helps to recognize how much you need to adjust your pace of life, to slow down to accommodate the slower rhythms of the person with dementia. This includes trying to see that "there are no interruptions." Life is now a procession of events woven with unexpected demands. Try not to label them as interruptions.

* Notice how you may have developed a new mode of

being aware. Perhaps you've developed more openness, sensitivity, and readiness to respond. Appreciate this as the practice of awareness—of being awake and present—considered a spiritual practice by the religious traditions, if you choose to see it that way.

* It is well known that living with serious illness creates tremendous strains on any relationship. It can eclipse all that has gone before and leave two people seemingly shackled together in a heartbreaking form of mutual imprisonment. How do you respond to the strains and stresses? Can you find ways to nourish your life apart from your responsibilities as caregiver? Can you reach out for more help? Experiment with breaking old stuck patterns of how you do things. Arrange to meet with a friend once a month or more; try to set up regular meetings to relieve the effort of reaching out anew each time. Spend time in nature. Try a new activity: start a hobby, take a course, do anything that's different and fun.

* Identify healing elements in your life. Know what nourishes you and gives you joy: your children or grandchildren; a creative activity like writing, drawing, singing, or gardening; your pets; a good book; or something as ephemeral as the way the sunlight falls into the room. Allow yourself to be nourished by these things, and notice how easy it is

to forget them when you're overloaded.

＊ While acknowledging the exasperating, harrowing moments, remember to affirm what is special and enduring about this relationship. What is the destiny you have shared? What difficult, recurring patterns are there to work through and, hopefully, heal? It's important for everyone to try to complete unfinished business before it's too late.

＊ Remember that caregiving is as hard as anything you've ever done. Whatever happens—and we know all the unpredictable, alarming things that can—the most valuable response is your steady, calm, and caring presence.

Seed Thoughts

I need to take care of myself.

Let me practice calm awareness for both of us.

May I appreciate our special moments.

CHAPTER SEVEN

PLACES NOT PREVIOUSLY VISITED

While some of our friends fell silent in the face of dementia, I welcomed those who did speak up. They gave me reality checks. A few close friends shared with me their impressions of Hob. Their observations helped me mark unfamiliar territory.

"There is a transparency and aura around Hob that suggests he's in a new transition," observed one friend thoughtfully. "You can see it in his smile, in a gentle warmth that surrounds him."

And there was Alice, an old friend who had a wise approach to just about every facet of life, no matter how difficult.

"For everything that slips on this side," she said with a chuckle but in all seriousness, "perhaps we gain on the other side. In subtle form, it may be like building a ship to sail into your new life. Maybe it's the opposite of what happens for the infant who builds bit by bit on this side and gradually forgets the other."

It had always struck me how readily people, when trying to talk about the mystery of death, speak about "this side and the other side," as Alice had. Her words felt right; Hob was clearly in a process of disconnection. The capacities of his mind were being disconnected, quite literally, and accompanying that was a sense that he was letting go on levels beyond the mind. There were the subtle intimations of this, but far more dramatic was the fact that we never knew what the next loss might be or what upheavals it might create in our lives.

One foggy evening a few months after my conversation with Alice, Hob and I decided to walk to a neighborhood restaurant for dinner. It was early November and already dark by six o'clock. The street lamps cast their light into the yellow leaves of the maples. The play of light and mist transformed the trees into a golden glow. I commented on the magical light effects but otherwise we walked quietly, hand in hand.

The restaurant was tucked downstairs below a little garden on a quiet side street. The walls were lined with brightly colored prints, all themes from France: landscapes, canal scenes, parades, dancers, still lifes of food and wine. Each table had an arrangement of fresh flowers and a flickering candle. We settled into a table for two in a back corner of the restaurant and moved into the leisurely ritual of being out for dinner.

Those days, given Hob's sensitivity to noisy, confusing environments, I was grateful that we had come early. Our meals together were quieter now. He sometimes initiated the topic of conversation, usually a well-worn one with which he was comfortable, but now I was the carrier of conversation. And there were many long, comfortable silences between us.

"Remember that time . . ." He paused for a long moment and looked away. He was gazing distantly at the wall opposite our table where there was a landscape of deer grazing at the edge of a meadow.

"Thanksgiving in Vermont," he continued. "We heard the rifle shot and saw the deer fall in the meadow beyond the driveway. But it was only wounded. Bad scene."

The scene flooded into my mind. The rifle shot. The flailing deer. The wild curiosity of Ethan and Laura who were still very young. Running to the window. Watching Hob run across the meadow. Yelling. But we couldn't hear. Watching the boy lift the rifle again. I could feel the flickering of outrage in my gut.

"How could I forget that scene, Hob," I replied. "You running out to confront the hunter who turned out to be a teenage kid . . ."

But I stopped. Hob's head had dropped toward his plate. He had slowly, inconspicuously slumped forward as if to brace himself against some passing pain. He remained bent over, silent.

"Hobbie, are you okay?" I reached across the table and touched his arm. No response. "What's happening?" I implored.

I shook his arm gently.

"Hobbie, are you okay?"

He was motionless, curled over in unconsciousness. I realized that he had passed out. I beckoned to the waiter. His face softened with compassion as he listened to my explanation.

"Oh, Ma'am," he said, putting his hand on my shoulder. "I took care of a man with Alzheimer's. I know a lot about it.

I'll get him a cold wet cloth for his head. May help bring him back." And he hurried off.

I felt like I had slipped into another reality—time suspended, every moment an eternity. Waiting. Breathing deeply. Everything charged with an extraordinary clarity as if I were being given the last moments of my own life. Wondering what to do next.

With my hand still on Hob's arm, I marveled at how discreetly he had lost consciousness. He had simply fallen forward. Why hadn't he fallen off the chair? Maybe, just as quietly, he'd return to consciousness. I sat there breathing deeply, holding on to that hope, distantly aware of the hustle and din of a restaurant now at the height of its evening.

When the waiter returned and gently began administering to Hob himself, I realized how much time had passed and said, "I think we need help. Let me take over, and get someone to call 911."

Unknown to me someone had already called for help, and within minutes the restaurant, already so small, filled with emergency medical people. Dreamlike and strangely calm, I moved amidst this sudden confusion knowing exactly what I had to do: get into warrior mode. Stay with Hob. Protect him.

As they carried him up the steps to the garden, which we'd come down less than an hour before, I tried to take in the scene outside the restaurant. It was surreal. Two people must have called 911 simultaneously, for there was an excessive gathering of emergency vehicles: two ambulances, the rescue truck from the fire department, and two police cars with their lights—blue, red, and white—spinning out alarm, ricocheting eerie light patterns off the surrounding buildings. It was like walking into a bad movie.

Along with the calm, I felt tremendously protective of Hob. I barked orders at those good-hearted souls, the EMTs. I exhorted them to leave him alone. No fibrillation, no ventilators, no excessive steps, because, I explained, he didn't want any of that.

"Lady, we have to follow our protocols."

No, they wouldn't let me ride next to him; that was against their rules. As I climbed into the front seat, I spun around. I was relieved to see that the front section opened into the back of the ambulance so I could watch what was happening. I was ready to throw myself over the seat if they started anything invasive.

It seemed an eternity since Hob had lost consciousness: it had been fifteen or twenty minutes. Still no sign of his reviving. His face was ashen. He lay absolutely still. I thought to myself, *Maybe he's dying right here, right now.*

One of the EMTs was vigorously shaking Hob's shoulders, shouting at him.

"Harrison, can you hear us! Can you hear us!"

I could see that he was beginning to stir ever so slightly. Something about the faint movements in his face suggested that he was straining toward speech. Then I heard him say, "Will you guys keep it down. I'm trying to die here."

The EMTs glanced at each other in astonishment. There

was a pause, and then the head man resumed his beseeching. "Harrison, are you in pain? Are you in pain?"

I could see Hob was trying to gather himself again, as if hauling himself up from some deep, distant place, struggling to come up with more words. He opened his eyes, looked directly at the head EMT, and said, "Everything's beautiful and nothing hurts."

A quote from a Kurt Vonnegut novel.[1] I couldn't believe it. Literary references, even in these circumstances! He had often quoted this phrase, words one of the characters had chosen to have inscribed on his tombstone. Somehow in the midst of the most perilous moments, Hob continued to respond with some unexpected, humorous twist.

⁂

After a brief hospitalization and the usual tests, inconclusive once again, he began reflecting on what had happened that evening.

"I was going to all these places I haven't previously visited," he said. "And now that I've died once, I can use that as my guide. This passing out, it's simple. There's nothing scary here. Not a big deal. In fact, it's just fine. If dying is this easy, no problem."

I was impressed with the ease with which he talked about it. He even seemed to take delight in the discovery that in spite of the chaos spinning around him—the state of emergency, the ministrations of the EMTs—what he was experiencing was manageable. He was conveying something about the ordinariness of death or the ease of the near-death experience.

After a few moments of silence, he spoke again, casually dropping one of those statements that struck me as an eternal truth.

"You can't live without doing a lot of dying along the way. You've got to get in the habit of letting go."

While not minimizing the reality that death is awesome, he regarded it as a natural part of life. Like breathing in, breathing out, every breath an inspiration and an expiration. Still, there was a vast distance between talking about his near-death experience and whatever might lie ahead.

For me a new chapter had opened. How could I continue to orchestrate our lives as I once had now that he might pass out anywhere, anytime? I went alone for a consultation with Hob's doctor. He explained that fainting spells sometimes occurred in the later stages of dementia. He called them vasovagal episodes where the blood pressure plummets and the pulse can become very faint. In Hob's case, he also became ashen and cold. When I asked the doctor if there was anything that would be helpful, he explained that there wasn't much to do but ride them through. He did give me some ammonia capsules, however, saying they might help to bring him back to consciousness faster. Primarily he encouraged me to keep doing all the activities that had enriched our lives all along—concerts, theater, eating out, taking trips, and so on.

So now, in addition to shepherding Hob through these

events, I became the vigilante. Everywhere we went, I assessed places for what would happen if he lost consciousness. Did the seats have arms? What would happen if he fell forward or sideways? How far from the aisle were we? How could EMTs get him out? Where was the nearest exit? A waterfall of questions and contingencies!

Heart pounding, I would sit through the first phase of an event juggling my need to be practical and foresighted with my desire to be present. In spite of all I knew about stress management and relaxation and working with the mind, I could not stop the momentum of catastrophic thinking as I inwardly prepared for another episode. Gradually, this kind of vigilance started taking its toll. My nervous system ratcheted into high alert, disturbing my sleep, deepening my fatigue. Sometimes I felt stretched beyond anything I thought imaginable, but I was determined not to break.

———— ∞ ————

"Dear Rinpoche, Could we talk about the subject of death?"

That was how I began the letter. I was sitting at a small oval table in a retreat cabin at Domo Geshe Rinpoche's place in the Catskill Mountains. I had come for six days. It was just after Hob's second passing out episode.

The word Rinpoche means "teacher" in Tibetan. I had met him a few years before at a time when I was still recovering from spiritual disillusionment, having spent many years in a meditation tradition which had refused to acknowledge its own darkness, a source of suffering to many former devotees. He was a hidden teacher. No scene around him. No public teachings. There were only two other people there. Ann and Danielle helped him to run a beautiful place beside the Beaverkill River, to which people found their way to be in his gentle, quiet presence. I trusted Rinpoche as a spiritual friend, and considered his place to be one of my refuges. I felt as though he had extended a compassionate wing over me—which he did to everyone.

I had heard that the Tibetans and Chinese rarely asked questions of him, but my friend Margot, who had known him for many years, explained that if you wanted to receive any teachings, you had to ask. Given how persistent the subject of death had been for me, I had decided to write a letter to clarify my own thinking and explain the issues to him ahead of time. I wrote in my cabin during the retreat as a way of getting to the key issues.

Even before he got Alzheimer's disease, my husband had said that he didn't want to "hang around"—that means "stay alive"—if he were in a vegetative state or a coma, obviously on his way to death. Recently he's been asking, "When is it time to go? When has the quality of life so diminished that death may be the noble way to leave?"

It may seem early for me to be concerned about this, but I have good reason to be. This disease attacks the part of the brain where decision-making, insight, learning, and judgment reside. He has already lost a lot of mental ability.

I pray that he will never have to make that decision. Yet as his ally in this, I need to face the issue with him. Of course we know the Buddhist teachings and have taken the first precept on non-harming. But we also come from Western culture where "the noble way," as it is sometimes called, of leaving life may be acceptable under certain circumstances.

The Dalai Lama has said each case must be dealt with individually. He said that it is difficult to generalize; the state of mind of the dying person is the essential factor. Harrison may still be quite a long way from physical death, but the mind is steadily dying. Another Tibetan lama has said that the wish to end one's life is the wish to end suffering—therefore it is a karmically neutral act. But is it, I wonder? Would he be creating negative karma if he chose to die before the body died naturally?

I'm wondering about my responsibility if he makes that choice. And finally, I wonder if there is a helpful practice he could start doing now. I would need to do it with him because he would forget. Or maybe there is a practice I could do for him.

I'm humbled by the complexity of all this. I also trust the mystery of however it will unfold, but I would welcome a chance to talk about these things with you.

I signed the note, relieved to have contemplated the issues and written them out. Maybe it was enough to have prepared inwardly, I thought to myself, as I tucked the letter into my journal and prepared to go off for a walk through the fields and woods beyond my cabin.

The next morning I walked over to have tea with Rinpoche. Our conversation started with the subject of the deer who wandered fearlessly around the place. They would come up to the house in search of handouts, usually apples which they ate from Rinpoche's hands. I told him about my encounter the day before with a doe down by the river who had allowed me to approach her ever so slowly, my hand extended holding a clump of meadow grass. For her, it had been a delicate dance between furtiveness and trust until that moment when I felt her soft muzzle pushing into my palm as she gathered up my grass offering. Feeding a deer in the wild. An amazing and deeply moving experience.

I moved on to the subject of the letter. I hadn't delivered it. I explained to him how Hob had started to talk about death and the possibility of an early way out. I told him that I was perplexed about my role in this and how to support him in whatever he might decide.

When I paused, Rinpoche replied quietly, "It all depends on a person's nature, on their fortune."

That's all he said. He didn't take a position. He didn't elaborate. His simple statement reoriented me to the perspective I had held, then lost several times during those last few years. Naturally what Hob decided and chose to do was a matter of his destiny. Yet because he had invariably turned to me to discuss the issue, I ended up entangled in his situation. His impairment had also contributed to my feeling responsible for how it would play out.

Rinpoche's statement was like the gentle adjustment of a ship's compass. Now it was a matter of trust for me. Reflecting on his answer, I saw the invitation to have faith. Ultimately, the remainder of Hob's life would unfold in accordance with his nature and destiny. I no longer had to shoulder the burden of responsibility that I had unwittingly taken on.

Rinpoche went on to talk about practices that could be helpful for this time leading up to death. He offered a form of light visualization which I could do for Hob that would help. It was a more specific form of the clear light meditation for the dying that I had trained in many years before.

As we talked, my feelings of burden dissolved. Thanks to the days of retreat and now our conversation, I could rest more easily. When I left and headed home, I had no idea of what lay ahead, but felt accompanied by trust and compassionate holding.

⁂

Life settled into steadier rhythms even as the days were marked with unexpected shifts and turns in Hob's mental states. One summer afternoon some months later when we were in Vermont, I came home to find him standing by the little front garden, waiting for me to return. He began to talk rapidly. He was clearly in a state of acute anxiety and paranoia. Urgently he explained to me that there was someone in the house, a stranger armed with a gun. "We can't go near the house," he said, "and we've got to do something about it right away." Everything in his face and body screamed with anxiety, shouted out alarm. I wondered what had catapulted him into this state. Where was Barbara, his companion?

I took his hand and gently led him a few steps away toward the sheltering white pine at the edge of the driveway. Perhaps if I moved him a few steps, it would help to soften the grip of his current state. Standing right next to him and holding his hand, I tried to help him unscramble fact from illusion, fear from reality. These mind-states were powerful, as if some channel of thought convoluted into fear and wouldn't let any other channel open until something stronger broke into it. As was often the case, the best strategy was to distract him with some diversionary activity. I suggested that we go to the front porch to have tea and watch the sunset together. That prospect apparently was strong enough to break the hold of the paranoia.

As we watched the play of color in the western sky, Hob broke the silence.

"I feel so fragile. Will you stay with me and see this through until the end?"

Tears prickled at his question. I could feel his sense of isolation, his fear of abandonment. I leaned forward and wrapped my hands around his.

"Of course I will. I know you're anxious when I leave to do something, but you absolutely have to trust that I'm here. That I'm your ally. I'm not going anywhere. I'm using all the heart I have to make this thing work for us, but you've got to keep trusting."

"I don't think I'm doing this too well. I just want to find home."

"You mean the ultimate home?" I asked.

"Yes," he replied, seeming relieved.

We continued to talk about the idea of *home*, a conversation we'd had several times before, mainly in the context of our hospice work where people talked about wanting to go home. Often *home* seemed to refer to some place of freedom beyond the struggle. I told him we couldn't know what the timing would be, and we'd have to trust that somehow we were being held in this journey. I shared with him that during the hard times, like today, I remembered the wise ones who had touched our lives; that I liked to think we could call upon them in some way; that we could ask for help.

"For surely, Hobbie," I said to him, "we can access the benevolent energy of those who have died before us. There's inspiration in doing that."

I began naming our teachers. I started with Father Bede Griffiths, one of Hob's two central teachers. Father Bede was a Benedictine monk from England who, in search of "the other half of his soul," as he described it, had moved to Tamil Nadu in southern India to spend the second half of his life at a Hindu/Christian ashram called Shantivanam, "Forest of Peace." Hob had gone there on retreat several times. He had become close to Father Bede, a man of wisdom who wrote and spoke eloquently of the mystical unity that underlay all the great religious traditions.

I also mentioned Howard Thurman, who had presided at Ethan's and Laura's naming ceremonies. And Ramana Maharshi and Anandamayi Ma—well known Indian saints who had inspired us both. Even Lise Ceresole, Hob's beloved mentor who, at a turning point in his twenties, encouraged him to go with her to a Quaker work camp.

Perhaps, I said, by remembering these wise ones we can tap in to that same source within ourselves. "We've got to trust that we can do it together, because otherwise why are we in this together?"

His expression had softened, signaling some lightening of his mood. We were sitting quietly now, watching the sky deepen in color. The mountains had darkened under the falling light. The stillness of evening cloaked everything in silence. At that moment an indigo bunting, fairly unusual in the valley, landed on the bough of a white pine about fifteen feet away. The bough danced in response to its delicate weight. I pointed to the bird as it rested on the branch long enough for us to get a long look. How often nature—the ultimate balm—came along to soften the ragged moments.

※ ∞ ※

Sometimes it took me a while to realize how Hob's unpredictable mind-states were affecting me. For example, it took me a long time to realize that I now lived in a "looser" reality than before, where the boundaries between sense and nonsense were blurred, where words obscured more than they revealed, where

185

time, place, and fact could all be hopelessly confused. Something was letting go in my awareness.

I could see that Hob's questions and repetitions were his threadbare connection to reality. His words were his lifeline. He still had fun with the absurdity of sounds, random consonants and vowels running together in wild combinations. Why should everything have to make sense all the time? Why always this linear, rational way of speaking? Sometimes that seemed to be what he was saying.

Other times, the playful reality turned upside down. His words carried an urgency that we—the verbally proficient—couldn't begin to appreciate. In a conversation late one evening, I could sense his determination to convey something exceptionally important. Thwarted by each incomplete phrase, he kept stopping and starting until finally he managed to say, "It's unfriendly because it makes you feel cut off . . . I'm trying to chase it away . . ."

"Well I'm doing everything I can to stay in touch with you, that's for sure," I answered in an effort to reassure him.

"I'm afraid. It's terrifying. If I stop now, maybe nothing in the morning, either." Of course he kept talking. Words—almost any words—reassured him that he could still say something. If he stopped talking, then there would nothing. Just the abyss of silence and separation.

"I'm dropping out of consciousness," he said, a clear statement finally emerging from the scrambled phrases. I tried to take in the full force of what he'd said—a highly intelligible analysis of where he was in that moment. There was also a finality to his words that I'd never heard before.

⸻ ∞ ⸻

We live, unwittingly, in a world of assumptions: that people will make sense; that they will do certain things; that we agree about time and place; that we can understand and be understood. But when all that unravels, where are we? My answer for Hob and me would be that we lived in an open, shifting, spacious reality where everything was undefined and totally unpredictable. "Isn't that the way reality is anyway?" you ask.

No, this felt quite different. This was a totally new experience. When I was rested and in balance, it was compelling—even exciting—because it was so alive and immediate, a perpetual wake-up call to live whole-heartedly in the moment. Meanwhile, it came to me as a revelation that amidst all the losses, the essence of this man I loved was still very much present. Sometimes my own preoccupations obscured my seeing, but astonishingly there he would be—the wholeness of his spirit shining through—his acuity, his sensitivity, his playfulness and humor, all intact. For example, there was a moment after he'd been entangled in some simple, practical task when, out of his confusion, he quoted something from his literary repertoire.

"There are things in heaven and earth, Polonius, that are undreamt of in your philosophy."[2] And then he added, "And if I laugh at any mortal thing, 'tis that I may not weep."[3]

These two phrases, both of which he had quoted periodically

187

over the last few years, expressed the heart of what he was experiencing. I thought it amazing that he could so graphically describe the trials of losing his ability to communicate.

"The words get stuck," he declared. "I've got this galloping brain drain. I know what I want to say, but the word horde is locked up. It's like a corral filled with horses, all pushing against each other to get out, but they can't find the gate. Now that's a good image!" he said with a laugh.

Without doubt, the humor that Hob brought to his situation was a gift, yet the nature of the disease had us both ricocheting between extremes—from laughter to fear. How could I answer him when he asked:

"Can you come back from this strange land from which most don't return because the words are gone?"

Hearing the edge of anxiety in his voice, I certainly didn't want to add to it. I didn't want to say, "No, you don't come back from that strange land." Indeed, what was it like to live in that strange land? He knew that land, because sometimes he was there and could speak about it. But what about the feelings of loss and desolation, the dissolving memories, the blanks, the disconnections?

"I don't know," I finally answered, as I moved toward him and maneuvered myself into an awkward, kneeling hug as he continued to sit in his green chair. We held each other for a long time, both silent.

When he didn't know where he was or what time it was or what was happening, the most effective way to ground him, to bring him back to reality, was through touch and action—taking his hand, walking to the garden, leading him to see the sunset. What was it like to be trapped in this labyrinth of mental losses with no exit? By now, wallowing around with words was usually a dead-end endeavor that led to heightened confusion and frustration. Could I stay open, I wondered.

Heavy rain was ricocheting off the window, lashing at the glass so loudly that Hob and I stopped talking to listen to the storm raging outside. We were sitting on the love seat in our Cambridge home before dinner, talking about our respective days. It was Thursday, Hob's day to attend the Boston Alzheimer's Center. The rain continued to drum against the windows when he began to speak.

"Some of those people . . . Pretty far gone. We talked about . . . what's it called? Started from that book. What's it called?"

"*Tuesdays with Morrie,*" I replied.[4] "Yesterday we worked out a question for you, about the growth that can come with aging. About learning to bring acceptance and understanding to your situation."

"Oh, right," Hob said. "I said so far it's been a pretty good ride for me. I'm planning to jolly well get over it. People do, don't they?"

Surprised as I was by his relative coherence, the question hung, reverberating, between us. I took a deep breath, wondering how to field this one. I couldn't believe that at this stage of things he still entertained the possibility that his disease was reversible. Nor could I believe that with his periods of rampant confusion he could still come up with as thoughtful question as this.

"Well, no, actually they don't." I replied.

"It's a degenerative disease," I continued. "Morrie had it in his body. He had Lou Gehrig's disease which progressively attacks the nervous system, but for you it's a degenerative process that affects the brain, the mind—another kind of trip. It is hard, really hard sometimes. Remember my mother? She ended up in a nursing home because her situation was so difficult. She needed that kind of help."

I listened to what I was saying, weighing whether I'd found the delicate balance between speaking the truth and protecting him. One part of me didn't want to state the reality of things this starkly, but this was how it was. Anything else would have been prevaricating, yet conversations about his illness were more of a challenge for me now. I knew the power of words to unsettle him.

"Then I'll be checking out early." He sounded strong, clear, and determined.

"If it gets hard, you think there's some way to check out?"

"I'll stop eating or something." A long pause between us.

"That's one way," I replied. "That's what my father did. Remember? Maybe you remember that day when he decided to stop eating."

"I'll do that. No late stages of this."

Another great gust of wind and the sound of pouring rain

suspended our conversation. We sat, listening to the storm. I let Hob's words sink into my awareness. We talked about death now as we might talk about plans for a day's outing. What psychological mechanism allowed me to be so detached? Denial? Or had I accepted where we were and where we might be headed? After all, we were now living in the last chapter of his life, of our lives together.

Some part of us cannot believe that our loved ones will die, even less that we ourselves will die. However much we reflect, read, and talk about it, the mind and heart struggle to comprehend death. In recent months I'd found myself rehearsing what life would be like when Hob was gone. I would eat breakfast alone while he still slept, or sit up late after he'd gone to bed, and impress upon myself that this was what lay ahead. He was gone. I was alone. It was in the natural order of things. That was what happened to fifty percent of everyone in a coupled relationship, as my father used to say, as a way to accept my mother's death.

⚬⚬⚬   ⚬⚬⚬   ⚬⚬⚬

In spite of Hob's clarity during our conversation that stormy night, one morning shortly after I was struck by the realization that he had long since crossed a continental divide. He was more in confusion than in clarity. I couldn't believe how long it had taken me to recognize that.

191

Changing Realities and Letting Go
Reflections

* With this illness, it becomes increasingly challenging to connect with the elusive world of dementia. We no longer inhabit the apparently secure world of consensual reality. As caregivers, we need to keep letting go of expectations and be with whatever is happening. The unexpected becomes our constant companion.

* You will find yourself in tricky situations where you need to find the balance between speaking the truth and protecting the patient. What feels right to you may be different at various stages and moments in the illness—something that takes sensitivity and skill.

* There is an old saying that we aren't given anything in life that we can't handle. Or to put it another way, we seem to find the strength to rise to the circumstances that life presents to us. This becomes increasingly true with advancing Alzheimer's. On some level, we are constantly being asked to let go and have faith—a very tall order.

* Whether the subject of death comes up directly or not, understandably many conflicting thoughts and feelings may arise for caregivers. Some will choose to remain quiet with the subject, or need to talk openly, or read something on the subject of death and dying (see Selected Bibliography), or share in a support group. At least it's valuable to recognize how death increasingly becomes our companion.

Suggestions

* As the patient's situation becomes more complex (anxiety, paranoia, repetitious questions, dramatic physical or emotional episodes), it becomes increasingly important to cultivate patience, steadiness, and calm. In many ways, we need to marshal all our forces of equanimity to counterbalance the wildly swinging states they may be experiencing. This in itself is a kind of practice; it will benefit both of us more than we may appreciate.

* Besides letting go of expectations and accepting ever-changing circumstances, it helps to realize that we live in a free-fall world governed by the unpredictable. Since both patient and caretaker are on a parallel journey, it can be comforting to say something like, "We need to trust that we can do this together." That statement validates the patient—regardless of how impaired he is—and reassures him that he is not alone, that you are in this together. Some patients need to be reassured of your loyalty to stand by them no matter what happens.

193

* For some people, the role of faith will be central throughout illness and death. For those less spiritually inclined, it still may be helpful in difficult moments to mention dear friends, mentors, or wise ones from one's past or spiritual tradition. At the least, it's a way to distract them from a troubling state; at best, it may provide them the comfort of feeling some connection to someone they love or admire.

Seed thoughts

Whatever happens, let's trust that we can do this together.

May I accept even death as part of life.

CHAPTER EIGHT

THE BIRD THAT SINGS
IN THE NIGHT

My father died the way he lived. In fact, dying was his last project. He approached each new undertaking in his life as his next project. He brought to each of them a wonderful combination of enthusiasm, intentionality, and will. He was an impressive role model in many ways, if at times a bit daunting. It should have been no surprise to us, his four children, that he would approach death with those same qualities. But it was a surprise: he had avoided the subject of death in just about every other way. He refused to go to funerals, even of close friends, and told us that he just imagined they had moved to Florida.

Tall and patrician, with blue eyes both piercing and gentle, my father, whom we called "Ammie," was a man of action and a leader. He was accustomed to being in command of situations. He had led a successful life. *Successful* was one of his favorite words. His conversations were peppered with it, and it might apply to anything from a major speech to a quiet family dinner. He approached his causes with a steady, burning passion and was accustomed to making things happen—big projects like directing Lincoln Center for many years, to little projects like writing a diatribe about the need for wildflower meadows versus chemically-maintained lawns.

Several years after the death of our mother, Ammie fell in love with Lucia. She was eighty-five, he was eighty-nine. He delightedly wrote a letter to each of us that sounded as if he were in his twenties again. Within a week of making the decision, he married Lucia and they moved to an elder community a few minutes from where Hob and I lived.

By the time Ammie was ninety-four his lifelong robust health was in rapid decline. This hit me particularly hard because Hob was now in his own accelerating process of decline. Ammie had cancer—he'd been diagnosed several years before but had refused most treatments. As someone who had a very determined mind-over-body approach to health, he never spoke about having cancer; the times I asked him about it, he always replied that he never had any pain so why think about it.

Now that he was failing fast, our family was concerned about how he would handle being an invalid. How does someone so fiercely independent surrender to the prospect of having his body cared for by strangers? I came to visit him the day after a hospital bed had been moved into his sunny bedroom. The windows were filled with flowering plants that Lucia lovingly attended. Given his rapidly deteriorating condition, I was scrambling to keep up with the latest changes. I sat beside the bed, holding his hand, trying to accustom myself to seeing my father in a supine position. The whole situation felt strange and topsy-turvy to me. He who had always stood so tall, presiding over events with his strong, dignified presence, now lay there quite still—the fallen warrior, virtually helpless.

He slowly turned his head toward me and said, "I've had a good life—a very blessed life—but it's over. Everything in my body's going. It's time for me to die. What are we going to do about it?"

The pronoun *we* jumped at me. I assumed I would be close to him to the end, but this close? I knew, however, exactly what he meant; he wasn't going to wait around for some long, lingering death. Not if he could help it. It just wouldn't fit his life plan. But then death never accommodates anyone's plans.

He clearly wanted to talk about his options. How could he help himself to die? Surprised as I was by his initiating this conversation, it turned out to be straightforward. One option—that of fasting—appealed to him. At the end of our conversation he said simply, "I am going to think about it."

The next day Ammie announced that he would fast. He asked how long it would take. That was an impossible question to answer, but I promised I would do some research, especially about how fasting related to the process of dying. Many people, in their last weeks or days, eat less and then stop, allowing nature to take its course, a gentle way into death. Still, it was difficult to find much information. There were stories, but they were variable in how long the process took. They seemed to agree, however, that it usually took longer than people expected.

The first few days of his fast showed that Ammie was living relatively easily with his decision. He was taking only fruit juice and water. He told us he was content and peaceful. During my next visit, he announced that he had now been fasting for seven days. In fact it had only been three. Yet it was obvious that he was continuing to hold his intention to die very strongly.

Those of us around him felt grateful that, except for moments of irritation with caregivers and family, he was handling each day with a lot of acceptance. My sister Joanie and I were both immersed in this new reality of my father's dying. We would brainstorm each day's situation, then weep together. We vacillated between admiration for his courage and grief over his impending death. We cheered him on and didn't want him to go. I felt numb. Then very alive. At some level I was ready to let him go. I even welcomed his decision. At the same time I recognized that we're never ready for our parents to die.

With each day it was apparent that he was quieter and sleeping more. He was also increasingly sensitive. He became cross if anything around him was rushed and explained, "My mind is working at about one-third the speed of yours." With his few words, he assured us that he felt peaceful and had no pain. Now he was taking only water, no more juice. About this time Hob came out for a final visit. He sat down beside Ammie's bed and reached for his hand.

"Good to see you," Hob said. My father turned his head slightly toward Hob.

"Hi Hob. Really good to see you."

"I came to say goodbye," Hob said simply. They sat together for a few moments in silence, father and son-in-law in their last moments together.

"Thanks for coming. You're a good friend," my father replied, and the two of them fell silent again. Giving Ammie's hand a last squeeze, Hob rose to leave.

A wave of tenderness came over me as I watched the two of them. Then sadness. They had always been very fond of one another. Hob had a special way with my father. He basked in Hob's banter and teasing and direct ways of speaking.

Invariably now, as each of us got ready to leave, Ammie would turn his head slightly to tell us that he loved us. Softened by his physical decline, his natural tenderness seemed now to be in full bloom. Except for his occasional flurries of irritation, which were totally understandable, it was very sweet to be with him.

In the days after Hob's visit, Ammie kept asking for reassurance about whether the fast was going all right.

"How am I doing? Am I doing all right?" he would ask. It struck me as both childlike and heroic that in the midst of this passage he could articulate his worries about how he was doing. He had always been one to expect himself and others to do their best. Now he was carrying that standard of expectation into his own dying process. Yet, how understandable. He'd never fasted before and none of us knew how it might go.

One evening I sat by his bed, my hand gently resting on top of his, that large, beautifully proportioned hand that had done so much in life. Memories began to surface, especially one from his late years where I saw him sitting at the piano in our music room, playing for hours, as he did every morning, filling the house with music.

Then, after a long silence between us, he said slowly and very quietly, "Dying—I'm on my way."

"Yes." I paused. "Death seems very close . . . We're cheering you on . . . We're letting you go . . . It's all going very well."

By that time, everyone in the family had come to be with him. The circle felt complete. All of us felt gratitude, even amazement, at how peaceful he had been. Even the moments of irritation at our speediness had subsided. He simply continued to become quieter, then almost impossible to understand, then silent.

That evening Lucia called to tell us that our father had died peacefully several minutes earlier. His fast had lasted only thirteen days. He had approached it as he had everything in his life—with determination and will. As he had said several times in those last weeks, he had had many blessings in his life. Now he had the blessing of a good death. Had he lived two and a half more hours, he would have died on exactly the same day of the year as Evvie, his first wife, our mother.

One cold fall morning after breakfast, Hob rose slowly from the table and sought out the sunny corner of the family room, as was his habit, where he sat, dreamily soaking up the sun. This was usually a quiet time for him. He seemed content, happy to be in his warm pool of sunlight. Silence was becoming as much a companion now as our exchanges of words.

Out of the silence, out of nowhere, Hob began to recite some lines of poetry I'd never heard him quote before.

Be near me when my light is low,
When the blood creeps, and the nerves prick
And tingle, and the heart is sick,
And all the wheels of Being slow.[1]

I felt tears rising. His words were wondrous and timely, like both a pronouncement about his state and a beseeching to me. "Be near me when my light is low." He went on.

"I feel time running out," he said. "Becoming mute. That's what I'm becoming. That would be very isolating . . . lonely."

I sat quietly, listening. Recently I'd noticed how my facile responses to him sometimes derailed whatever tender track he was on, so tenuous and delicate, as if he were trying to feel his way tentatively through some overgrown path through the woods. In contrast, my ease of speech was like a train lumbering down a track. His words reflected something that I'd begun to notice—some deep sea change in our lives together. Was it that his death was more imminent, or was it because illness slowly transforms the life you've known and prepares you for the inevitable great passage?

I could feel his vulnerability. The words "mute and lonely" reverberated in my heart. I asked him if he would recite the lines again. His face brightened. He repeated the lines, this time with additional gusto.

Every couple of months I spent time with Ildri, a friend and gifted therapist whose husband, many years younger than she, had died after a prolonged, complex illness. More than any of my friends, she knew intimately the complexities of caregiving. Norwegian by birth, Ildri embodied the finest qualities of a Nordic warrior—grounded, steady, powerful, and direct. A tireless explorer of psychology and healing, she was an incomparable ally during challenging times.

On cold winter days, as I settled into a comfortable brown leather chair, she would wrap a multi-hued blue blanket around my legs and invite me to plunge into whatever feelings, images, and associations were up for me.

"Okay, Ildri. Let me start out with a dream, because all along they've been signposts that show me what's really going on."

I am traveling on a road which goes down into a valley where suddenly it comes to a place where it is flooded with water. The water is too deep to drive through. I can't go on. I have to stop and appraise the situation. I simply don't see how I'm going to get to that next place that lies ahead around a corner.

I ask some people who are around how they would get across the flooded road. They come up with various solutions, but none of them seem possible to me.

I paused for a moment. I could feel the impact of the dream images in my body. Aware of my sadness and the cold, I wrapped the blue blanket tighter around my feet and continued.

"That's it right there—the way life feels these days. I can see where I'm supposed to go, but the way is flooded. *I'm* flooded—

all the responsibilities, all the ways I need to respond and help him. Most of the time I sort of know where I'm going, but right now I feel as though I've been stopped by the flood."

I continued with a stream of associations: wishing there was someone to put a protective arm around me; longing for someone else to take over the responsibilities; grieving over the lost vividness of my husband; longing for my own mother; lamenting that I had to go through Alzheimer's for the second time; recognizing that even with these vulnerabilities there were still blessings in the midst of it all. The ten thousand joys and sorrows called life. Nothing special. Just what everyone else experiences sooner or later.

As the dream indicated, there wasn't any one solution. There was only living moment by moment, day to day, opening to the unknown, welcoming the new, embracing whatever happened. Embracing? That wasn't always possible. Most of the time, however, I experienced a finely-tuned awareness that arose in response to the delicacy of some interaction we were having. There was a constant call for creativity. In my strong moments, I appreciated the opportunities of our journey. In my vulnerable moments, I wondered if I could hold up through what felt like an interminable march toward death.

What sustained me more than anything else was my faith in meditation and the teachings. I knew that all the teachings were there and that they would support us through whatever came up, no matter how challenging or harrowing. All I had to do, for example, was to remember the *paramitas*, or perfections, of Buddhist philosophy—six qualities that can be cultivated for inspiration. Just to name them made a difference: generosity, discipline, diligence, contemplation, wisdom, and patience. Reflect on them; cultivate them; pray for them, I'd remind myself, for they were a blueprint for how to live life. At this point in Hob's illness, generosity and patience were in highest demand. Every day involved countless moments where his needs came first, where just to remain present and responsive involved generosity. And then there was patience. Surely it was one of the primary tests of living with someone with Alzheimer's.

Although long since removed from our refrigerator, for many years a poster had been taped on the freezer door right at eye level. It was an announcement for a workshop on patience offered by a Buddhist group. Emblazoned at the top of the flier in large letters were the words "Patience: The Armor of Non-aggression." Underneath were undulating blue lines in bold brush strokes that created a wavelike design, powerful and serene at the same time. The image intimated that patience was not something mild or passive, but strong and steady, even courageous.

At the time, as a young mother faced with the perpetual challenges of child-rearing, I needed that sign! I needed the constant reminder that patience, not reactivity, was an option. Now, living in very different circumstances, the words and image—indelibly imprinted in memory—came back to me. I actually made a practice of invoking that image of the bold blue lines, a visual reminder of the power of patience.

The *paramitas* in Buddhism, including patience, are qualities that the practitioner is encouraged to cultivate—indispensable steps in the process of freeing the mind from afflictive patterns. With this understanding, patience becomes an aspiration to hold in one's heart, a refuge whenever the fire of impatience arises. For impatience is a form of aggression: against oneself, against the other, against the space in which it erupts.

I realized how familiar the surge of impatience had become these days, with its heat and ragged edges, its insistence and righteousness. Sometimes even the twinges of martyrdom. Sometimes spilling over into raw frustration and outrage. Primitive! Overwhelming all of my best intentions! Lost it again!

Much of the time I was able to catch it, that moment of awareness that could observe the rising fire. I remembered the breath. Then another breath. Back into the body and this moment—the only moment there is.

So many times awareness rescued me from the rising fire of impatience. I knew it was caused mostly by strain, fatigue, and tedium. Because of our situation, my feelings of impatience were strangely impersonal. They were triggered more by the circumstances than by Hob, who, because of the nature of his illness, was obviously not responsible for whatever provoked me. I chuckled with recognition when I came upon a classic teaching story about this phenomenon.

On a river in Southeast Asia, a boatman is ferrying his passengers to the other side. It is late in the day. The light is falling, the shadows deepening. An evening fog has rolled in, obscuring the far shore. The boatman and his passengers strain to make out the faint shapes that take form and then disappear in the foggy twilight.

Suddenly through the fog they see another boat approaching from upstream. It appears to be on a collision course. The boatman yells out: "Watch out! Watch out!"

No answer from the other boat. It continues to approach as the anxious boatman and his passengers watch, helpless, in anticipation of the inevitable collision.

Again the boatman yells, his voice coarse with anger: "Change course, you idiot! Watch where you're going! Watch . . ."

The boatman abruptly stops. As the other boat comes close and the fog thins, he realizes that there is no one in it. An empty boat. His yelling has been for naught. He reaches out his pole and fends off the empty boat, then watches as it slowly drifts on downstream.

And so it is, living with dementia, the boat is empty. The impatience rises against the situation, not the person. It rises against the powerlessness, the frustration, the grief. None of what was happening was Hob's fault. It was just the way things were now. Accept everything, I reminded myself, including the precariousness of his life at this point.

⸺ ❧ ⸺

The next precarious moment wasn't long in coming. It had been a hard winter with a series of Northeast storms, each one arriving with high winds and heavy snows, temporarily dislocating life along the New England coast. On this particular evening, snow was again falling heavily. The storm had followed the previous one by only two days, and there was already a heavy cover of snow everywhere.

Old friends had driven in from the country to join us for the evening. We had gathered at our house to share a leisurely dinner before leaving to attend a performance of Bach's B Minor Mass. The snow, spiraling and dancing against the outside light, added a festive, adventurous aspect to the evening. As we headed out into the night, already we were bracing against the storm, cleaning off cars, brushing snow off clothes, all of us wondering if we could get to the concert and home before travel became impossible. It was Maundy Thursday, the night before Good Friday. Somehow the weather seemed eminently appropriate to this time in the liturgical year.

This was to be a landmark concert performed by one of Boston's leading choruses and led by a brilliant young conductor. We arrived early so that we could hear his pre-concert talk on the B Minor Mass, a piece of music Hob and I both knew well and which Hob had once sung as part of a choral group many years ago.

As the conductor concluded an inspiring talk, our anticipation for the concert was even more heightened. There was still, however, a long wait while the rest of the audience arrived. As the orchestra warmed up, the energy level in the theatre continued to rise. I became aware that Hob was growing restless. He looked around, reacting viscerally to the cacophony of sounds. He flinched at the noisy greetings of friends, the loud outbursts of laughter, the shrill sound of instruments rehearsing. I moved closer, took his hand, and quietly reassured him that this pre-concert pandemonium would soon be over.

Finally the music began with its sublime introduction, the orchestra leading us into the ravishing beauty of Bach's music. We were sitting high up in the mezzanine, near the aisle, in a dark part of the theatre. These days whenever we were at a performance of some kind, I had gotten used to glancing at Hob inconspicuously to make sure he was all right. About fifteen minutes into the performance, I noticed that his head had fallen slightly forward, his eyes lowered or closed. Was he listening? Sleeping? I kept watching. Then squeezed his hand. No response. I shook him gently. No response. He had passed out.

I had already been through my pre-concert scanning of our surroundings. Whispering to my neighbors, I asked if they could move to create enough space for him to lie down, for praise be, we were sitting on cushioned benches without any armrests between the seats. I figured that if his body were level with his head down, perhaps he would regain consciousness as he had before and could lie there until the intermission, when somehow we could get him out of the theatre. But he didn't respond to my gentle shakings or whispered words. As the minutes went by, I sensed that this was the most serious episode he'd had so far. We had to get him out of the theatre as soon as possible.

Although this was happening quietly and discreetly, the people around us knew there was a crisis. The manager soon appeared beside me and asked if he should call for help. Yes,

I said, and tell the EMTs to turn off their intercoms, because I knew they were taping this concert. Strange, the details that surface at a time like this. Once again I was in the hyperaware, calm state that descended during these crises. As the great Mass played on, monumental and dramatic, Hob was quietly carried out of the theatre into the windy, snow-driven night, and into the waiting ambulance.

The questions and protocol were all familiar to me by this time. I made as strong contact with each member of team as I could. I knew that I had to connect with these people personally in some way if they were to hear my request. I was back in fierce, protective mode, asking the EMTs to take him home, not to the hospital, a nightmare place, I explained, for someone with dementia.

"Lady, we have no choice. When we're called, we're obligated to take the patient to the hospital."

I bought time. I invoked every tactic I could think of. I told them what had happened the last time Hob spent the night in a hospital. Finally the head technician said, "If he can tell us himself that he wants to go home, not to the hospital, we'll see."

Hob lay there motionless, strapped to the gurney. He was silent, his eyes closed, his face sepulchral. Again, he looked as if he was at the edge of death. He was unconscious so how could he possibly speak? But somehow he must have heard what was going on—my insistence, their reluctance.

With eyes still closed, his voice sounding thick but audible, he said, "Not the hospital. Take me home."

It was another victory. Small in the great scheme of things, yet what strange, juxtaposed realities we lived through that evening: the sublime music, the wild storm, the helpful people, the edge of death. I experienced all this with heightened awareness, combined with the now familiar altered state of consciousness that arose in those extremely stressful circumstances. The generous, skilled EMTs took him home, carried him upstairs, and helped with every detail, including sweeping out all the snow they had tracked into the house.

In response to my call, our son, Ethan, arrived to help. That was the most moving time of the whole evening. I watched my son care for his father. I watched, helping around the edges, as Ethan gently bathed him, helped him into his pajamas, held the glass to offer him water, lowered him carefully into the bed.

That evening the generations reversed roles; Hob was as helpless as a child, Ethan was the strong, tender parent. Having never seen Ethan in a situation like this, I watched, deeply touched by his protectiveness, sensitivity, and compassion. It was a balm on all the strain of the evening.

After he had settled Hob into bed, Ethan stayed on to hear the evening's story. He knew that I needed his company as well as time to unwind from a dramatic episode. It was deep into the night by the time I collapsed into sleep, restless and disturbed by wild dreams. The snow continued to fall outside. The sounds of the city became muffled, everything quieted under a foot of fresh, new snow.

"I was someone else last night, so it's hard to find myself this morning."

That was Hob's statement the following morning. Even with his limitations, he persisted in trying to describe his inner world.

"Oh how all occasions do conspire against me," he continued, his expression warming. He looked pleased with himself. Shakespeare again.[2] What a brilliant way to describe how last night had been for him.

It usually took Hob a couple of days to recover from these episodes. He spoke less, moved slowly, and slept a lot, as if going into hibernation to restore himself. When he did speak, it was either about something practical or else he continued to process the event with occasional statements or by reciting verse of some kind. His statements came out of nowhere.

"Tell that guy [the EMT] that he brought me back from the dead, unwittingly perhaps."

He'd ask me to tell him again what had happened, as he struggled to assimilate the events.

"This disorientation is different every time," he observed. Starting to chuckle, he pulled out an old expression he used to cite when life seemed to be too difficult or complicated.

"Get in bed with your hat on; that's the best solution!"

Later that day, he began singing one of his favorite songs, a ballad that he used to play on his guitar.

So if you see me passing by,
And you sit and wonder why,

And you wish that you were a rambler, too,
Nail your shoes to the kitchen floor,
Lace 'em up and bar the door,
Thank the stars for the roof that's over you.
And I can't help but wonder where I'm bound,
Where I'm bound,
Can't help but wonder where I'm bound.[3]

Where was he bound? Where were we in this journey? Sometimes I would remember our first Zen teacher, the Korean Zen master Seung Sahn, who had lived for a while at a small center just a block from our house. We used to go over for dharma talks when he was teaching. There he would sit on his meditation cushion at the front of the room, dressed in his gray robes, presiding over a room full of eager, often perplexed students. He sat like a mountain, emanating steadiness. At the same time, he twinkled like a kindly uncle who was having a tremendously good time.

Seung Sahn's teaching style consisted of raising one impenetrable question after another. The purpose was to surprise our rational, linear minds into an experience of spaciousness and freedom. Only when the mind is free of its usual array of concepts, opinions, and patterns can it open to the truth of things so often obscured by rationality.

After someone had been stumbling around for an answer, the Zen master would break into a radiant smile, lean forward slightly, and in his Korean accent would say emphatically, "Only don't know! Have don't know mind!"

He spoke with a combination of force, detachment, and

delight. Having "don't know mind" was one of his central teachings. It was unforgettable because of how he delivered it. Hob and I used to mimic him to each other. We'd exaggerate his posture and articulation, a surefire way to shift from seriousness to humor.

Now here we were, very much living with "don't know" mind in a "don't know" situation. Both of us in different ways were in a process of surrender. Needless to say, I didn't always remember the wisdom of surrender, but I experimented spontaneously with various phrases that helped me to cultivate an attitude of surrender. "Let go . . . Breathe . . . It doesn't matter . . . Relax . . . Stay open . . . Soften around this . . . Just be with it . . . Accept this . . . Just this moment . . . Again, let go . . ."

And there was faith. Faith was somehow partnered with surrender. Faith that we'd make it through. Faith that at some level, no matter what was happening, everything was going to be all right. Faith that somehow we were being held by everyone around us—family, friends, strangers, and the *sangha*, our meditation community—seen and unseen. Somewhere I'd once read, "Faith is the bird that sings in the night while the dawn is still dark."

SURRENDER, TRUST, AND END OF LIFE ISSUES
Reflections

* It's often observed that people tend to die the way they live. If someone has lived a life of hurt and anger, those tendencies may continue to the end of life. If they've been strong-willed and controlling, then those patterns may prevail throughout. On the other hand, life-threatening illness can create the conditions for dramatic change: a cold, judgmental father becomes gradually more mellow and accepting; a long alienated parent/child relationship seems miraculously healed. Anything is possible in the realm of human behavior, especially when serious illness starts to soften and break apart rigid patterns. We need to be open, ready, and accepting of whatever forms the behaviors may take.

* It's common knowledge, but hard for some people to accept, that as a final illness deepens, the patient may start to eat less or refuse food altogether—a voluntary form of fasting. We need to accept how natural this is, the body's way of hastening and easing the process of death. Yet the issue of food can turn into a battleground. We can ask ourselves, especially if the patient is unable to speak, what might her wishes be? If there is conflict between what we want and what the patient may be trying to convey, how are we going to respond? Whose wishes are we going to honor? Eating less or refusing food is often the body's natural response to illness. Perhaps it also signifies the patient's unspoken decision to start letting go of life. Whether spoken or unspoken, are we ready to support them in that decision?

✳ When someone is nearing the end of life, one's sense of reality may be shaken to the core. It's like being in totally unfamiliar territory in the midst of daily life. We may become distracted, preoccupied, irritable, or forgetful. We may feel as if we are living in heightened or dreamlike states. Or we may feel very present at times but disconnected, distant, and adrift at other times. We may have troubling, vivid, or numinous dreams. We may experience unfamiliar or altered states of consciousness.

Death is always a wake-up call to the preciousness of life, yet it may also be profoundly unsettling and frightening. Our humanness is laid bare. Most importantly, we need to trust that these are all natural responses, and that we're in a process that will find its own resolution over time.

✳ Consider reflecting on what the word *surrender* means for you. It does not mean resignation or giving up, but rather it suggests letting go and trusting the moment, whatever arises. An attitude of surrender invites a sense of strength and ease. It suggests having faith in something beyond your limited self, something that helps when you're living with forces beyond your control. As long as you are in community, it's trusting that end-of-life issues magnetize family and friends to hold you through times of greatest brokenness.

Suggestions

* We tend to get most upset by the things we take most personally. When the fires of impatience flare, remember that it's mainly the situation not the patient that triggers your heated reactions. Impatience is fueled by feelings of powerless and frustration. Just acknowledging that helps. You can also play with shifting your perspectives: how would this situation look a year from now, or from a distant city, or from the moon? Humor helps to unravel the tightest knots of feeling, including impatience.

Here are some practical reminders, some already mentioned earlier.

❖ Remember the breath, perhaps repeating the word *calm* or *ease* or *peace* as you inhale, letting go of strong feelings or tension as you exhale.

❖ Choose a photo or image that evokes peace and happiness for you, and place it in a conspicuous place.

❖ Repeat *patience, patience* silently to yourself,

and imagine that you are creating a calm energy field around yourself and the other.

* Remember how important it is to know what rescues you in times of need. As mentioned earlier, don't forget your rescue list, and review some of the coping skills discussed earlier.

* Since unexpected crises are bound to arise, families are wise to discuss possible contingencies ahead of time. Do you know what the patient's wishes are in regard to critical care? Does she have a health care proxy, living will, and/or medical directive that expresses her wishes? Copies of these documents should be in the files of the primary care physician, family members, lawyer, and in an emergency file, preferably bright red, in a conspicuous place in the patient's home.

If you plan to care for your loved one's body at the time of death, have you researched the information you need? Have you familiarized yourself with your state's laws on this subject and contacted a funeral director ahead of time? (See "Caring for Loved Ones in Death" at the back of this book.)

As our physician reminded me, even the best-laid plans can still be thwarted by unforeseen medical circumstances. Nevertheless, it is wise and comforting to know that you've addressed these issues as thoughtfully as you can.

✳ The immanence of death has a profound impact on everyone. This is the time for connection and support from the family members and/or friends that you can most trust to be with you.

Seed Thoughts

Give me strength for whatever happens.

May I listen deeply for what the patient wants.

CHAPTER NINE

AMBUSHED BY THE UNKNOWN

"Now I can feel it. I'm nearing the finish line of life. Things are getting weirder and weirder. It's all so delicate—this thing of being alive—knowing what day it is, who's where."

Hob was sitting on the blue stool in the kitchen looking out at the stand of hemlock trees outside the window. It was the sixth summer since he'd been diagnosed, and we were in Vermont once again.

In the last week he had started to have visions of things in the landscape that weren't there—the rock in the upper meadow that he swore was a buffalo, the partly fallen tree that looked like a man fishing, a green dog playing a violin in those same hemlocks by the kitchen. He was alternately persistent and perplexed, afraid and amused.

"It's a complete revelation to see myself evolving like this!" he exclaimed that morning and laughed. At times he expressed his anxiety and alarm at these episodes. But he could also shake his head with wonder and make some wry comment about the craziness of it all. In spite of the visual illusions and verbal deterioration, he still had the ability to be aware of what was happening to his mind.

He also could turn to me and say, "I'm very sorry to drag you into this business, but I'm very glad you're in it with me!"

Operating on intuition, sometimes I decided to go along with his visions in a playful way, whereas other times I took a different tack. I'd acknowledge his vision, describe what I thought I saw, and laugh about how elusive our ways of seeing could be. I developed so many strategies for responding to Hob's comments about the buffalo-shaped rock, I lost track. It was like some new children's game, except that the stakes for him were hidden and very high. That buffalo rock, visible from many places around the house, was about halfway down the meadow from the great maple. By that summer, only one valiant branch had managed to put forth a few leaves. Otherwise, our tree stood almost naked against the summer sky.

⚬⚬⚬ ⚭ ⚬⚬⚬

Since the passing-out episodes, the possibility of Hob's death hovered close. These incidents happened randomly at different times of day, in different places. His doctor said that they might continue for some time, and that we should continue to live life as before.

We did, but I noticed a deep shift within myself. I remembered several years earlier when I had developed what I called my "pathway practice," an inner preparedness for meeting Hob's latest crises whenever I returned home. Besides being a skillful exercise in mindfulness, it softened the shocks.

It fortified my patience and allowed my heart to stay open. Now, living with the imminence of death, a new practice arose, again spontaneously. I thought of it as my "doorway practice." Whenever I approached any doorway to a room where Hob might be, I was inwardly open to the possibility that he might have died. Curiously, there was nothing morbid or depressing about it. Rather, I experienced a calm awareness. My doorway practice quickly became instinctive. It was so natural, I slipped into it before any thought of it even arose. It was a kind of grace. That I knew.

It is said in the Buddhist tradition that even if you carried your mother on your back for your entire life, it wouldn't repay her for giving you birth. This may be classical hyperbole, but I find it a compelling image. The teaching is less about the issue of burden than a reminder of the preciousness of human life. We forget. The message is a wake-up call to startle us out of complacency, to stop taking life for granted.

Given the nature of our days, it was not surprising that I also identified with the karmic burden element of this image. I was aware of Hob's dependence on me. For anyone living with Alzheimer's, there is an obvious equation: the relentless process of loss creates an equal and opposite dependence which, of course, falls most heavily on the partner.

I was his grounding in a groundless reality. I was his port in the storm. I was the word finder, the one who intuited the lost train of thought. I was the one who held the structure of his days; the one who comforted him during night confusion; the one who knew the best medicine—touch and song.

No wonder his dependence felt heavy. After all the years of sharing a lifetime, I felt as though he was tugging at the core of my being. I could feel his vulnerability. I knew illness had slowly demolished his psychic shield, leaving him almost unbearably sensitive and unprotected.

Practitioners who do energy work describe the psychic threads of connection between two people who love one another. At death, the threads between them break. I imagined that in cases of dementia, those threads begin to pull apart earlier, as the psychic fields slowly disengage from each other. I could sense how some of the psychic threads of his being were disconnecting both from me and the world around him. A slow, ruthless process. I never knew when the tug of pain might come. It was like waiting to be ambushed by the unknown.

Yet much of the time I kept myself so busy I couldn't feel what was happening. I had soldiered on through so many difficult situations, I had unconsciously armored myself emotionally. These were the hidden dangers of this journey; my coping mechanisms might not always serve me well. Periodically I erupted with impatience or grief—the big ones. I exerted every bit of will to protect Hob from my intense emotions because of his sensitivity. If I was happy, so was he; if I wept or said a sharp word, he flinched.

As his illness brought more complexity into our lives, I

had to keep finding my places of refuge: time alone, walks, the garden. I discovered little rituals of renewal, like walking the path to the vegetable garden on late summer afternoons. Warm sun-baked grass under my bare feet, the air still except for the cacophony of insect life, and the sweet fragrance of milkweed that bordered the path. The garden was hallowed ground where everything grew, bloomed, bore fruit. Abundance everywhere.

I was reminded there that we, too, live in the cycles of nature. Nothing is out of order. It is not unnatural for someone in his late seventies to live with a degenerative disease. When I lost my perspective, a visit to the garden gathered me into the embrace of nature. At the deepest level, I once again knew that all was well.

Whoever would have thought that one of the most valuable teachings Hob received for the last phase of his life would come from a disabled man? His name was Leroy. He came into Hob's life some years before the memory problems appeared.

We had gone to hear a lecture by Jean Vanier, the founder of the L'Arche communities for the disabled. Vanier had been the son of the Prime Minister of Canada, and had started life with all the advantages. He became a decorated Navy commander, a university professor, published writer—a man gifted in many fields. That night he talked about how, by the time he reached his mid-thirties, he felt that none of these accomplishments added up to a meaningful calling. Now in his early sixties, he was a tall, slender man with a shock of white hair. Something about his posture and the way he moved conveyed that he was gentle and strong, noble and humble. Kindness and compassion seemed to radiate from him.

As a devout Catholic, he knew he had to find a way of life that embraced the depths of his faith. He had already spent time with the forgotten people of the world: those with mental and physical disabilities. All but abandoned by their families and friends, they were often placed in institutions. Yet Vanier had observed that they seemed to be more in touch with the joy and mystery of life than the accomplished people he had known.

Vanier's vision became clear. He made a radical decision and took two mentally disabled men into his house. He went on to describe how their simplicity emanated a sense of sacred presence. He intimated that because their minds were impaired in various ways, they dwelled more naturally in their hearts: humble, gentle, and loving. He felt that they were closer to God than most people. He chose to live in community with them because they had the most to teach him. This man's bold experiment launched the first L'Arche community. Now with nearly one hundred communities scattered around the world, Vanier has created a loving revolution in the lives of the disabled.

Deeply moved by Vanier's presentation, Hob volunteered to spend a month as a temporary family member with "the special people," as they were called, in a L'Arche community in Erie, Pennsylvania. When Hob arrived at the L'Arche house, he was assigned to be a companion for Leroy, a man with multiple disabilities who was in his late forties and relegated to a wheelchair. It was Hob's job to help Leroy with the simple, daily activities of his life. One hot August morning, their household job was to clean out the refrigerator. As Hob told the story, he was crouched on the floor beside Leroy's wheelchair. He handed items from the refrigerator to Leroy, who slowly, laboriously placed each one on the counter. Everything about the task seemed to move in slow motion. At one point Leroy paused to look out the kitchen window. His attention had been caught by a man striding by on his way to work. Clearly the man was in a hurry.

"Hob," said Leroy in his halting voice, "they say we're handicapped," and he tipped his head in the direction of the man passing by outside.

He paused as he reached for his next words. That gave Hob enough time to wonder, a bit nervously, what was coming next.

"But I think *they're* handicapped," Leroy continued, referring to the man who had just passed by. Gently he tapped his hand against his chest.

Hob wasn't sure what Leroy meant.

"Oh, you mean, they get heart attacks?" Hob guessed, assuming that Leroy was making reference to hardworking, type-A personalities.

"No," replied Leroy. He paused again, slowed by his difficulty in forming words. Then came the memorable statement.

"They don't know how to let love in," said Leroy.

This statement was to reverberate through Hob's life for the next ten years. He said that it had been the one teaching he most needed and most valued.

⸎ ⸎ ⸎

When Hob returned from the L'Arche community, he tried to convey some sense of what the experience had been like for him. We were sitting at the table in our family room having a cup of tea.

"When I first got there, I didn't know if I could stand it." That's how Hob began. "But these disabled people touched notes and chords of affection in me that I'd never felt before. They had qualities that defy description. Especially generosity—great generosity of heart. It's almost enviable the way they take care of each other, how they pray together, free of so many things that we struggle with, like resentment and anger."

He paused, took another sip of tea, and continued.

"Just because Leroy is in a wheelchair doesn't mean that God is off duty. In the face of all that adversity, the folks at that place know how to celebrate the littlest things, how to celebrate every day. We could learn from them!"

He went on to explain the link between his meditation practice and caring for the disabled. "I couldn't have done that work if I hadn't done those long retreats where life slows way down and one has a chance to look really deeply into the nature of things—one's own mind, life itself," he said.

"At L'Arche, I finally figured out what it is that they have, and it's pretty close to the top of the line. They have open hearts," Hob said. "How do you take a course in *that* at a university? Or how do you take a course in wisdom? They're not in the catalogue! Can't take a course in how to have a spacious mind and an open heart, or how to have a sense of humor."

Hob continued, "And such sweetness and thoughtfulness. When anyone visited there, the L'Arche folks would remember them years later and pray for them. They carry a lot of people in their hearts, even the people who have hurt them, like their parents, and still they pray for them.

"These people had one thing in common; they'd all had their hearts broken, often and regularly. There's great beauty in the wound that opened up—the wound of the open heart."

He paused. He was holding his mug reflectively.

"I don't know about you," he continued, "but my heart isn't always open. Is anyone's? Mine needs to be broken open. Regularly! That's what Leroy did with those words when he said 'they don't know *how* to let love in.' That's my assignment and it's a big one!"

Those words turned out to be the most compelling message for Hob's last years. I came to think of it as one of the two signature stories for how he handled the decline into dementia. The first had been the experience of forgetting his talk: what he had described as the death of pride, the death of ego—both indispensable in the process of letting go.

Hob was to tell the Leroy story over and over again. He told it as a teaching story in his meditation classes. He told it to friends who came to visit. He told it in France at his ordination ceremony. Prophetically, Hob talked about how we need to open to the care and help of others, how we need to let go of our fierce independence and, above all, let go of our pride.

How to let love in is an archetypal theme. It becomes an urgent call when any of us—deeply attached to our independence—need to be cared for by others. We may deny others the gift of their generosity because we aren't comfortable with receiving or because we feel that we don't deserve it. In Hob's case, expressions of love from his family in his early years had been painfully missing; he survived by becoming independent, sometimes stubbornly counter-dependent. Then he was a therapist and teacher, always giving to others. With his illness, the equation turned upside down; now he had to let the love in. He recognized the challenge. That explained why he told and retold the Leroy story. When he could no longer remember the sequence of what had happened, he would turn to me to fill in the lines. I knew the story was like a golden thread for him, a connection to a teaching that he needed when everything else was dissolving.

Years later I tracked Leroy down to let him know how his wise words had touched many hundreds of lives on two continents. I could hear him weeping at the other end of the phone.

———— ⁂ ————

Once again I had gone downstairs for the night in hopes of getting uninterrupted sleep. It was early dawn when the door opened and Hob slowly came in. He climbed awkwardly into bed beside me. I felt my entire being collapse energetically. Once again—ambushed by the unknown. How could I possibly begin to handle anything to do with him? I felt only exhaustion and desolation.

"I've got to make some plans," Hob said, his voice heavy with discouragement. "This isn't working. I've got to get out of this."

"What isn't working?" I asked. I tried to hide the impatience that had suddenly woken up, too.

"All these people around. Every time the car starts, it's you going off again. What am I supposed to do? I've got to do something else. Something different from this. How can I get away from it?"

"Hob, we need this help. There is no other way for us to do it now. I've got to keep going in my life or else I'll break. You know what happens to people who are sole caregivers. They often get sick. Sometimes they die. I'm not willing to do that."

There was a pause. I was gearing up inside, trying to strategize beyond the agitation that had taken me over. In the dim light, awakened from sleep, trapped in the narrow bed, I felt as if I was lying in a hellhole.

"How can I help you?" he asked. His tone of voice had changed dramatically to concern. His shift of direction startled me. I struggled to shed my dark thoughts in response. How had he done that, he who had been so desolate a moment before? I guessed that my desolation had driven his away. We had always delighted in what we called the "well-bucket principle" in our relationship; when one was down, the other went up, and vice versa. That way there was always someone to help the other one up again.

"You can help by accepting our helpers. Letting them help you, because I can't do it all," I told him. "The truth is that we're living in a world of impermanence. Remember? And it's hard, really hard. Our lives are changing. Our relationship is changing. We need to let each other go more than ever before. I never thought about it before now, but I know it's true, even if it sounds harsh. I know it's probably easier for me to say, but you've got to trust that I'm totally with you even if I leave to lead my own life. My heart is totally with you. You've got to trust that."

I was struggling to hold back my tears. I'd never spoken about this before. It hadn't occurred to me. It was such a new thought—a major realization, in fact—that I was surprised by my own words. I now knew that from some greater perspective it was time to begin to let each other go. I knew that our relationship—even with all the love—would disengage slowly now from its old forms. Maybe this was the most loving thing I could say right now. It was the truth, wasn't it? For him, the bearer of this disease, it must have sounded like another form of abandonment. This was hard. Still feeling shaky, I continued.

"Remember the de Chardin quote about the grace of diminishment? How in his youth he said he thanked God for his expanding life, but in his later years when he was declining he thanked God also for what he called the grace of diminishment. I think we've got to do our best to live this gracefully. I think that's the call for both of us."

"Yes, that's what we're being asked to do," he responded.

As we lay together in silence, I found myself reflecting on my own words. How do you let a loved one go?

AMBUSHED BY THE UNKNOWN
Reflections

* As the challenges increase for us as caregivers, how can we accept that the difficulties, sorrows, and heart-breaks of illness and aging are a natural part of life? For instance, can you look beyond the outer appearances of what's happening—the deterioration, confusion, tedium—and see what lessons might be hidden in the hard times? I was being forced to grow in new ways: I developed heightened sensitivity and intuition to deal with difficult situations; I deepened in love in ways I couldn't have imagined; I learned to trust that compassion for myself and others could embrace any-thing—even death.

* The concept of the sacred dimension of aging is radical. It is both counterintuitive and countercul-tural. Nevertheless, it is truly worth pondering. If we are to normalize our culture's attitudes toward

aging and death, we need to accept that end of life issues can encompass ruthless polarities from painful, intransient illness to potential transformation, emotional and spiritual. Death can be a powerful teacher, enabling or forcing changes that none of us could have anticipated.

* For both caregivers and patients, dependence issues may become increasingly amplified. Asking for and receiving help can be really challenging, especially for those in the helping professions or the fiercely independent. Reflect on your feelings about dependence and see what comes up when you say, "I need help."

Suggestions

* No matter how inwardly prepared we may be, or think we are, the prospect of a loved one's death seems unreal and elusive. For me, what I called my "doorway practice" (the readiness to enter a room to find that my husband had died) kept the possibility of death very present in a positive way. It heightened the preciousness of life. It made me feel receptive and tender toward him. Quite simply, it was realistic. However you handle this phase, some combination of openness, readiness, and acceptance will serve you well.

* Even if it is obvious, review for yourself and other helpers what seems to help the patient the most—the

best "medicine" for him—and make sure he is getting plenty of it. For Hob it was music, walks, watching golf on TV, and touch. For my mother, a lifelong reader and writer, it was holding a book in her lap—her anchor to something familiar even though she could no longer read.

* Conversely, be vigilant about what disturbs the patient. This becomes increasingly complex as the disease progresses. So-called ordinary situations (such as negotiating stairs, confusing light patterns on the floor, loud noises) can throw the patient into alarm. Review the approaches of Rehabilitation Therapy and revisit the many practical suggestions in Alzheimer's books. I mention this because, with the demands of the later stages of Hob's illness, I forgot the resources that were right around me.

* Contemplate the phrase "the gifts of aging," if only because it helps to soften the aversion most people feel toward their aging. Consider the flip side of the aversion: perhaps we're being called to a more expansive, accepting vision of the inevitable; perhaps we can begin to let go of body images, limiting ideas about ourselves, and unreal expectations; perhaps we're being invited to grow wiser in ways we couldn't have imagined. These realizations can help us both personally and with the process of caregiving.

Seed thoughts

I can let go and love at the same time.

May I let love in.

CHAPTER TEN
GONNA' JUMP SHIP

The cooler nights of fall had touched the Vermont mountains with color. The maples were blazing red and orange, the birches gentler hues of yellow. At the edge of the meadow, the branches of the boysenberry bushes hung heavy with their deep purple fruit, a haven for migrating birds.

Hob and I had stayed in Vermont longer than usual to enjoy the fall season but for another reason as well. We wanted to visit a Tibetan teacher who was coming to a Buddhist center a couple of hours away. At that time one of our helpers was a student of Khandro Rinpoche, a well-known Buddhist teacher, and she wanted Hob to meet her. As with so many things in our lives now, every decision seemed fraught with peril. Would Hob be able to manage something that complicated? I would drive him for two hours to a place he hadn't seen in almost thirty years to meet someone for a twenty-minute interview. Was it worth all the effort it would take both of us in different ways?

I also knew how carefully Hob had threaded his way through the sometimes tricky territory of meeting spiritual teachers. By nature skeptical and questioning about teachers, he had invariably kept his own counsel in such settings. He scanned for power gone awry or for trouble hiding in the shadows behind the outward appearance of things. I imagined that he could balk at the last minute and want to come home. The Rinpoche was, after all, a woman far younger than he, even if she was highly regarded for her wisdom, humor, and gifted teaching. But now that life was so challenging for us both, I was ready to reach out for any offering of support. Maybe we would get another perspective on our situation. It definitely seemed worth the effort even with the risks for Hob: a long trip, a crowded meditation center, a new person to meet.

The day before the meeting, I suggested to Hob that we go out on our porch to sit in the morning sun, a favorite post-breakfast ritual for him. He was usually most cogent in the early morning. I thought that we could try to prepare for the meeting. I knew he couldn't formulate any questions, much less remember them, but perhaps together we could come up with a focal point for this meeting.

I sat down opposite him with a yellow pad and pencil on my lap.

"What are we doing out here?" Hob asked with a puzzled expression.

I reminded him where we going the next day. Maybe it would be helpful, I explained, if we prepared for the meeting. I coaxed him gently. He would speak, then pause, then look vacantly toward the meadow. As I waited within the silences, I became aware of the warming sun, the humming of insects in the goldenrod nearby, the wind gently stirring the willow's branches. I also began to feel the familiar sinking—my sadness over his gallant struggle to persevere through something difficult. After about half an hour we managed to formulate two subjects that he could raise with Khandro Rinpoche.

The next day when we turned up the steep driveway toward the collection of buildings, I couldn't help but see everything through his eyes. Partly this was the careful attention that I'd learned to cultivate in order to shepherd him through all we kept doing together. And partly it was my concern over whether the decision to come had been a wise one.

Hob and I were shown upstairs to wait in a hallway. There was the familiar scene: the heightened atmosphere around a famous teacher, the whispered anticipation of people waiting for their interview. In the past all these would have been triggers for Hob, but today he was quiet. His old patterns of skepticism and judgment had vanished under the determined hand of the disease. To my great relief, he seemed mellow and content.

When it was time for the interview, we were taken through the main interview room where the previous visitor, an autistic man, had fallen asleep on the couch where we would have sat. Instead, Rinpoche was waiting in her bedroom. Seeing me hesitate at the door, she invited us in with a warm welcome. She offered Hob a chair in the corner by the window and showed me to a second chair. She perched herself on the edge of the bed, the three of us sitting close because the room was so small.

The conversation began with pleasantries about the

wildflowers from our meadow which I'd brought as an offering. Although many Tibetans have a way of appearing ageless, Khandro Rinpoche was young, maybe in her early forties. She had an open, bright countenance, steady and serene. She struck me as a woman of authenticity and effortless power.

After a pause, I saw Hob fumbling with the yellow paper I'd just handed him. On it I'd written two questions from our conversation the day before. There was a long, easy silence. I watched for clues, attentive and ready to help him.

He looked up from the paper and started chuckling.

"I have this problem with my mind but I can't remember it."

I waited. Rinpoche waited. After several more moments of silence I quietly offered the word.

"Alzheimer's," I said.

"It's okay," Rinpoche responded in a matter-of-fact tone. "You have fewer problems when you have Alzheimer's. In Tibet many people have something like Alzheimer's—maybe the same—but it is never seen as a problem. Take it as part of the meaning of life."

"Never seen as a problem." She must be exaggerating, I thought to myself. Yet her statement echoed what Tulku Thondup had said to me several years earlier. I couldn't imagine what cultural differences could account for such divergent views—Eastern and Western ways of looking at diseases of the mind.

Another pause. Hob looked down at the paper again. He

was obviously confused. I could see that he wasn't able to make the leap from reading the question to asking it. I reached for the paper and read for him.

"The question is how not to cling to life when there isn't any more going on."

"Be happy in every moment," she replied without any hesitation. "You don't need to change anything. Let everything happen just as it comes. Just flow with it. It's the process; everything dissolves into you, so change with whatever happens."

He studied the paper again, paused, and haltingly read, "What practice makes it easier to let go of this life?"

"The best practice," she replied, "is calm abiding. Remain with the breath. Develop calmness inside. Join awareness and the breath. Trusting these. Trusting the knowing. Trusting the calmness. Not pushing yourself to make any changes. And not paying attention to what others say about it."

"That's not too hard!" responded Hob, breaking into laughter that carried us along with him.

Then, smiling tentatively, he said, "I'm wearing out."

"That's how it should be," she answered, throwing back her head and laughing with total heartiness, as if to say, how could anyone expect otherwise when you're an older person with a degenerative illness.

"I'm accused of cracking wise a lot," observed Hob, which precipitated another round of hearty laughter.

"We have a saying in Tibet," she answered.

"Beyond acceptance and rejection,

Beyond hope and fear,

One can't do anything else but burst out in laughter."

"Ah, that will keep me going," replied Hob. He looked very pleased. As someone who had always loved meandering conversations peppered with laughter, I could see that he was thoroughly enjoying this exchange.

There was another silence. Then Hob looked at her and added, "This reveals to me that there is a lot more in practice than some people think." I was amazed at his clarity, for he hadn't been this lucid in some time.

"Yes, and there's no reason for tensing up," Rinpoche replied. "Be easy with yourself. Just make your life big enough for yourself. Rest in the spaciousness."

Another silence. I sensed that the interview was coming to an end. Hob had asked his two questions, so I added my own.

"I've been reflecting on attachment a lot more lately—my attachment to him, to our lives together. I realize this is a huge opportunity for surrender and how to be free in the midst of it all, but it isn't always easy."

"You're both doing very well with all this," she replied.

Always figuring there's nothing lost in asking for something more, I said, "May we ask your blessings for this transition, for him and all of us around him."

She leaned forward slightly and with a faintly mischievous smile, she replied, "You pray for us and we'll pray for you, and we'll hope something works!" Once again we all laughed, and with a flurry of final words, thanks, and farewells, we left.

We retraced our way through the room where the man still slept, down the stairs, and out into the bright fall day. I glanced over at Hob. I could see from the relaxed, open expression on his face that he had enjoyed the meeting. He had risen to the occasion with observations and responses that kept the conversation moving along. I felt lighter, less burdened, more hopeful. Rinpoche had met everything about Hob and his situation as a natural part of life. Above all, she had affirmed how the fruits of his meditation practice could carry him through. She had given us an infusion of energy and inspiration at a highly opportune time. No question now that it had been the right decision to come.

⸺ ❧ ⸺

All along, Hob had been making observations about what he was experiencing, including a number of comments about dying or death. He was fortunate that so far some part of his awareness remained intact, which was unusual at this stage of the disease. At the time I thought little about the stages of Alzheimer's, but if asked, I would have said that he was in the late middle stages.

"I just wish I could go into the light," he said to me the day after our visit with Rinpoche.

He paused, his expression sad and reflective, and then added, "I feel as if everything is out of joint in the world and me."

We were sitting on the porch on a radiant September afternoon. We'd had a series of beautiful days where our mountain landscape scintillated with light. Yet the coming of fall brought

241

moments of melancholy for me. All this beauty heralded the end of summer, the fall of light, the coming of winter.

By now I had learned to wait and be silent after Hob spoke. He had once told me that the process of mental loss was all about getting *"down* to speed," emphasizing the word *down*. Looking at me intently, he had repeated it several times as if he were training our dog, and then chuckled at his creative way of beseeching me to slow down to meet him at his tempo, not mine. No small assignment.

Still waiting, I turned toward him. He was dressed in what he called his uniform: khaki trousers, a faded work shirt frayed around the collar, and sneakers. I sensed a deep weariness in him, not just a late afternoon slump in energy but the weight of the illness. It was one of those moments of seeing deeply, at once poignant and tender. I realized that increasingly we lived in worlds that were drifting apart, like two continents being inexorably separated by hidden forces.

Finally he went on, speaking in fragments, pausing between each sentence.

"Somebody's here wearing my clothes. That's how I feel. I'm getting lost a lot now. Life's all kind of in the now. It's not going any place. It didn't come from any place. It's all the moment. Sometimes that can be a little scary." He stopped.

Into the silence came the clear, galloping call of the yellow-throated warbler, hidden in the mugo pines below the porch. Both of us remained still, listening while the little bird repeated its brilliant, bold declaration to the world. Another silence.

Then haltingly Hob continued his ruminations. "I hear a voice saying, 'Leave him to heaven.'" Long pause.

"I really have to keep track of myself . . . of who I really am. But as soon as I wake up from this dream, I'll be in heaven."

His face, once animated and mobile, had lost its brightness, as though some hidden hand had erased all traces of feeling from his expression, robbed him of all liveliness. How incongruent, then, that he could still come up with these vivid statements about his state.

I could see in his eyes—in the strain of concentration—that he hadn't finished what he wanted to say. Clearly he was struggling to complete some sequence of thought. Finally, with a flush of satisfaction, he spoke.

I warm'd both hands against the fire of life;
It sinks, and I am ready to depart.[1]

Another poetic fragment he remembered from long past, though I'd never heard him recite it before. He was graced; he could convey the depths of where he was with a couplet. That afternoon I didn't put together the various fragments of what he had just been saying, even though they all pointed in the same direction. Maybe it was denial or, more likely, my weariness from keeping up with his ramblings, lost words, and confusion.

———

A couple of days later we returned to Massachusetts, a tremendous dislocation for someone in Hob's situation. Familiarity of place and routine provide stability for anyone whose mind is going. But our brown shingled house in Cambridge had been our primary residence for over three decades. It was easier there to find the help we needed for Hob. I had commitments there to teach, counsel, and resume a meditation group and my ordination circle, which had both been lifelines for me over the last five years.

The meditation group had evolved from a lively meeting we convened to support our friend Charles, a minister from Oregon, who had come to Cambridge to create Elderspirit, a program for the elders in his church community. We had gathered a small group of friends who shared an interest in the issues of aging and spirituality. Our meetings, held in our living room, were a high point in Hob's world. I was grateful for the deep, caring support of these friends whom I trusted to stay close with us no matter how difficult Hob's journey might become.

A few days after we'd returned from Vermont, the group gathered together for the first time after the summer. We sat in a circle on the living room floor. There was a simple altar in the middle of the circle: a teal green cloth, a vase of yellow chrysanthemums from our garden, a statue of St. Francis, another of the Buddha, a Celtic cross, and a candle burning brightly.

After the pleasantries of coming together, I watched with some concern as Hob maneuvered himself onto his meditation cushion, no small matter these days when his balance was precarious, his coordination compromised. We settled into silence and the half hour of meditation. As usual, I kept checking on

Hob. At one moment, something made me open my eyes. In a glance, I saw that he was starting to fall forward. His face was ashen.

"Hob needs our help," I said quietly into the silence, and moved to support him while the others gathered round. Awkwardly, we half pulled, half carried him over to the couch where we arranged him as best we could and covered him with a blanket. The four of us were sitting on the floor around him, everyone's hands resting somewhere on his body. We were quiet, waiting. After some minutes, Hob began to stir. He opened his eyes, turned his head toward us, his brow furrowing with confusion.

"What are you guys doing there on the floor?" he asked.

"Just sitting with you," someone responded.

"Some trip. Never know what's coming next," Hob said after a moment, looking toward us with the trace of a smile.

"I didn't plan it this way," he added, then closed his eyes again. That much talking had exhausted him.

The rest of our time was spent on the floor around him. I figured that the presence of four loving friends was the best medicine for this situation. We lapsed into conversation, quieter in tone because of Hob's vulnerable state, but still light-hearted and reflective.

While relatively minor, that episode turned out to be the first of a series of crises that came in rapid succession. Over the next three days, Hob passed out five times, a dramatic turn in his situation. Even with two of us, our helper and me, we were no longer able to handle all these episodes. Obviously Hob was on a downward trajectory. Finally my back went out as I tried to adjust his body when he'd collapsed another time. We had no choice but to call an ambulance.

On the second day at the hospital, Hob had a massive stroke. From one moment to the next, he was stripped of the ability to walk, care for himself, or talk, except for the rare word or phrase that arose unpredictably from the stillness that had descended around him. Determined to get him out of the hospital as soon as possible, I scrambled to set up a twenty-four-hour care system. He was taken home, a fallen warrior facing into a new phase of his journey.

⁓ ⁓ ⁓

Quiet or asleep most of the time, Hob now lay in our living room in a hospital bed that faced out into the garden. Sunlight poured in through the sliding glass doors and over his bed. On the corner of the wooden deck right outside the living room, bright red geraniums still bloomed in their planters. Leaves floated aimlessly from the maple that shaded a weathered garden statue of the Buddha near the back fence.

One day soon after Hob was home, as I sat by his bed I was flooded with wondering. What had he experienced these last few days? What was it like to lose so much, so fast—the ability to walk, to care for oneself, to talk? True, he occasionally spoke a few words here and there, but language was no longer subject to his will. The words appeared at random, unpredictable intervals. He had vanished into a distant inner world, inaccessible to us. I longed to be able to communicate with him, but the best I could do was take his hand, embrace the silence, and try to intuit what he might be experiencing. I imagined his unspoken thoughts—what he would have said to me if he could have spoken, if his mind had still been intact.

You sit beside me. I can feel how you're struggling to be with me in this new situation. Surprising, but I feel peaceful. Accept this sentence. Waiting? No, not waiting. This is another realm of consciousness. Probably going toward death. That seems unreal, but it would be liberation from this. All I can do is surrender. Accept. Lie here suspended in time and just be.

Something protects me from understanding what's happening. Going this one alone. Suspended in liminal space—floating, drifting, searching for the familiar, but everything keeps dissolving.

Very quiet now, feeling far beneath the surface of things. Sometimes your hand here holding mine, but we'll have to let go of that, too, our deep, eternal connection. Drifting away.

⸙ ⸙ ⸙

We got a new system of helpers in place and gradually adapted to the new circumstances. Amidst the crisis, I could appreciate that this phase, while personal and unique to us, was shared by countless others—the universal experience of accompanying a loved one toward death. Remembering that the personal and universal are forever intertwined was one of the secrets to staying afloat in the middle of these challenges. The sources of support and inspiration were all around us. Laura, our daughter, flew back from China where she had been doing postgraduate training in Chinese medicine; my sister Joanie flew in from Oregon. Both came to help in the immeasurable ways that such times call for. Besides family members and friends, there were all the other outpourings of care: the messages, the flowers, the pots of soup, and the rotation of helpers who came to the house to care for Hob through day and night.

Two days after the stroke, Hob's neurologist called to ask if he could come by the house to see him. He had ordered another MRI, but given the severity of Hob's condition, we didn't want to take him back to the hospital. The combination of dementia, his previous hospital experience, and his amplified sensitivity made that an easy decision. I accepted the reality that whatever would happen was beyond my control. Nonetheless, if there was any way to keep him out of the hospital and let him die at home, we as a family were deeply committed to that choice.

After less than ten minutes of examining Hob, the doctor—a good friend after four years of periodic visits—explained to Ethan, Laura, and me that the stroke had hit the right hemisphere of his brain and parts of the left. That's what accounted for the paralysis of his left side and much of his right side as well. The doctor came up with a wide-ranging prognosis: Hob could die fairly soon, he said, but then it was also possible that he could linger on for several years. We should plan accordingly.

I felt strangely detached as he made this pronouncement. Maybe I was on automatic pilot. I wondered why I wasn't feeling more. Maybe it was disbelief or denial. By far the hardest part of the prognosis was the wide-ranging element of time.

I continued to put one foot ahead of another. I had no idea how long I could manage to live with the intense situation of Hob's being cared for at home. Two months, six months, a year? Only time would settle that question. Meanwhile, I searched out possibilities for the time, which might come, when his life and mine would be better served by his being moved to a long-term-care facility.

Within a couple of days, after visiting a small hospice house in our neighborhood, I felt reassured that we had found an ideal option. It was a brightly painted house on a quiet side street that had been converted from a single family home into a four-room hospice facility. Not only was it within walking distance of our house, but it had an intimate, homey feeling. It was an ideal option for when the time might come. I decided we would reconsider the situation at the beginning of the new year, about two months hence. Ethan, Laura, and I all knew that Hob would prefer to die at home. But the wild card was how long, even with help, I could manage the complexities of his current situation.

I thought back to the conversations that Hob and I had had periodically over the last six years. He had been clear all along that he would stop eating "if the going got rough," but what volition was left to him since the stroke? There was a vast difference between discussing such a weighty issue in the abstract, and how it might feel when you were right up against the reality of it. It was clear, however, that we were now living in the daily presence of the great mystery of death.

⸺ ⟨∞⟩ ⸺

Once again I returned to talk with my friend Tulku Thondup. It had been six years since my last visit. I appreciated that the Tibetan tradition has a profound understanding of how to approach death, and now I sought any perspective that might help Hob with the process he was in.

On previous visits we began with some catching up about our lives, but this time we quickly turned to Hob's situation and my concerns, especially what practices might be most helpful. T.T. offered a series of reflections that I later distilled into five seed thoughts, each one an invitation to remember something eternal that lay hidden in the details of caring for Hob.

"Our meditative practice is not only about improving life so that we can share our peace and joy with others," T.T. said, launching into his quiet, seamless way of speaking. "It is also about preparing for our death. Any kind of practice—whether it is prayer, devotion, or meditation—all improve our mental qualities which will guide us when, in the process of dying, there are no longer any physical or environmental supports.

"Prayer and meditation awaken compassion and open the mind to oneness—his mind, your mind, all minds. Try to unite his mind and your mind into that boundless, joyful peace of mind that will touch all beings. Remain there as long as you can. That is traditional tantric meditation: to visualize the world in this peaceful, boundless, joyous state.

"As you meditate and do your devotional practices, there will be calmness and light. Visualize his body and mind surrounded by that and then see it filling the whole room. Make prayers for him, for all suffering beings, and for the entire world which is going through so much turmoil.

"Visualize blessing light. See his body and mind filled with that blessing light. The room filled with it. All beings filled with the blessing light. Here is where all pain and confusion can be transformed into peaceful, joyful blessings.

"See him as a body of light. His mind is not entrapped now, but enjoying the peace and compassion of the Buddha. For you, stay in the peacefulness and light, and feel that he is enjoying the same, that all around him is filled with those qualities of peace, joy, and blessing light, all radiating out to all beings everywhere."

At the end of the visit, while I stood in the doorway ready to leave, he excused himself a moment and returned with two small packets of light brown paper. He handed them to me and said, "These are for Hob. One of them contains soil from holy places in India and the other has ashes blessed by several lamas. I send him blessings, and if you would like, I could come by to meditate with him when it's a good time."

"Thank you, we'd both appreciate that," I replied, accepting the packets. I knew I would put them on the altar that was on the table across from Hob's bed, but I sensed that T.T. intended them to be some part of the final ceremony we would do when

Hob finally died. But when might that be?

Most of the time Hob was silent, even when his eyes were open. The stroke had affected the language center in the brain. On the rare occasions when he spoke a few words, they contained only fragments of meaning. Sometimes there was the faintest twinkle in his eyes—his humorous streak remained intact.

A series of heart-warming events unfolded around him. Family moved in closer. Many friends came to meditate or visit quietly by his bedside. Other friends came by to play the guitar and sing. There was Noah, son of dear friends, who stood a little distance from the bed so as not to overwhelm Hob with sound, and played a series of Bach suites on his viola. My sister pulled Hob's guitar out of its case, and we spent several evenings singing a repertoire of old favorites, mostly songs from the 1960s and favorites from our childhood. Hob joined in sporadically, his voice a shadow of its once resilient form. It was clear that he was enjoying this sing-along.

Jocylyne, one of his principle helpers, a great-hearted, merry woman from Haiti, spoke Creole to him. He had led Quaker work camps in Haiti, and now here he was at the end of his life with Jocylyne who sang him Haitian songs, made him a CD of her favorite Haitian music, and coaxed him, at least in those first few weeks, to speak French with her. Hob had spoken fluent French, a language he savored and loved. French or English, she encouraged him to try to speak one word at a time.

"Not too many to spare!" he had replied, smiling wanly at her. Subtle as the changes in his facial expression now were, one could see that he welcomed her kind way of being with him. To me she was an angel who had dropped in at this critical moment.

Even the neighbor's cat joined the stream of visitors. Cleocatra, affectionately known as Cleo, was a calico cat, strikingly brindled in white, tan, and black patterns. She deviated from her usual detached perambulations through our garden and one morning insisted upon being let into the house. She pawed with determination at the full-length doors to the living room where Hob lay. Then, undaunted by our refusal to respond, she followed us to the glass doors of the family room. She had never done this before. Never had she been so determined and insistent.

When I finally let Cleo in, she went straight for Hob's bed. I gently placed her on his lap, where she settled contentedly, purring loudly, allowing him to stroke her with his right hand, the only part of his body that still had some mobility. He had always been a great lover of animals, but we no longer had either our dog or the succession of cats who had always graced our household.

She came regularly for about ten days. When I noticed one day that she had stopped coming to the door, I realized upon reflection that Hob had moved into a deeper, quieter, more sleep-filled place, and that her purring ministrations might have been an intrusion. We know that animals are highly intuitive, but how to explain these touching, timely visits by a steadfast neighborhood cat?

Only in the first week after the stroke could we, with elaborate maneuverings, get Hob into his wheelchair to take him outside on the deck to enjoy the Indian summer days. One day we had just finished getting him into his terrycloth bathrobe and slippers and wheeled him out onto the deck, when two old friends arrived. There was something heightened about the encounter that took place. Some flicker of life seemed to rekindle in Hob for those few minutes.

Arnie and Therese, who lived in Hawaii, were old friends from an earlier phase at Thich Nhat Hanh's community. Fortuitously, they had arrived in Cambridge for a brief stopover during one of their teaching tours. The moment Hob saw them, he reached out tentatively toward Therese, his right hand shaky and limp. He made a welcoming sound, deep with pleasure, as his face brightened ever so slightly. The faintest trace of expression had broken through the mask of dementia, the flattened appearance caused by the disease.

We all understood the common language which began to unfold in Therese and Hob's cryptic exchange, a series of fragments woven together by long, easy silences. Arnie had settled quietly onto the steps of the deck, while Therese was kneeling beside Hob's wheelchair. Her hand rested gently on his knee.

"Can you let go?" she asked him.

"Not if you're attached," he replied without even a pause. Then a muted chuckle—a more expressive response than he had been capable of for days. I was astonished that Therese's kind words had elicited any response at all, much less such a comprehensible one.

After a long pause, she went on, phrasing a question common to the meditative tradition that they had shared.

"Are you enjoying your breathing?" she asked.

Hob looked at her wryly, and replied, "You've got to be kidding."

Another long silence, and then surprisingly, because he rarely initiated words any more, Hob said, "A big ship . . ."

"Where is the ship going?" replied Therese.

Very slowly, Hob raised his index finger, pointing heavenward.

"Gonna' jump ship," he stated matter-of-factly.

"Are you afraid?" she asked.

"Yes, but it's time."

We couldn't have known it then, but that exchange between Hob and Therese was to be the last of his reports from the interior. Again, the clues were there. He had been remarkably clear with scarcely any words at all.

Reflections, Suggestions, and Seed Thoughts for chapter 10 are at the end of chapter 11.

CHAPTER ELEVEN

A GOOD DAY TO DIE

The candle flickered on the table across from Hob's hospital bed in the living room where I had assembled a simple altar. It was another late evening in a long procession of days. I sat on a chair next to his bed in the semidarkness of this welcome time of day. For me, this was a liminal time. I felt as if I were dwelling between two worlds: the physical world of Hob's care, now completed for the day, and the invisible world of his inner process. Jocylyne, his favorite helper, was reading quietly in the dining room. A deep calm had settled over the room.

He lay quietly, his eyes closed, his breath slow and regular. Behind him was a table with three plants all in exuberant bloom, especially the brilliant red Christmas cactus that was blooming almost two months early. Beyond him was the beautiful Japanese screen that I had brought home from my studio to place around the table that contained all the things necessary to his physical care. The smallest details were now of inordinate importance. Even though Hob lay there, his eyes closed most of the time now, I asked his caregivers to keep the space around him beautiful. This was not just about caring for his physical body. Every bit as important, I felt, we needed to be sensitive to whatever process Hob was in.

To my left was an altar composed of mementos from Hob's life. Candlelight played off the gilded surfaces of his favorite statue of the Buddha. There was a photograph of our grandchildren, Oliver and Andrew.

On the right side of the altar stood his favorite family photograph taken two years earlier, not the usual variety with everyone grinning broadly, but the subtle interactions between family members looking toward each other, not at the camera. The photograph portrayed a family gathering that would never be repeated, I realized—Hob would no longer be there.

Finally, next to the grandchildren, there was the photograph of Hob and Father Bede Griffiths, the man who had been his primary spiritual teacher. They stand together at Father Bede's ashram in southern India, a moment from Hob's last visit there ten years earlier.

Illuminated by the play of candlelight, the various images reflected treasured aspects of Hob's life: his family, his love of Vermont, and his inner journey which had spanned various traditions, especially Christianity and Buddhism. Past and present were interwoven for me as I sat quietly reflecting on the joys, the sufferings, all the permutations of our life's journey.

Now we lived in the midst of the great passage from life to death. Yet each day passed, as ordinary as the previous one. There was the ordinariness of cooking up pureed pears or mashed potatoes. There was the ordinariness of answering the phone, greeting visitors, or offering water through a straw. It was as if the ordinary world had telescoped to an intense focus on the living room and Hob's care.

At times I hardly felt up to the task. Time dragged. I was tired. The nights were long, robbed of deep sleep, filled with disturbed dreams. Still, some thread of assurance wove through the days. I sensed how we were part of a much larger picture. I would feel linked to all others in similar circumstances. I'd remember that there was nothing different or special about our situation. Countless people sat as we did, wondering, doing their best, waiting for death. Then the lens would open yet further to include all those experiencing helplessness in inner city ghettos, in refugee camps, in war zones. These compelling images link us to something beyond our particular circumstances, and I needed some practice with which to hold them. Then I would remember T.T.'s suggestions and visualize the blessing light, as he had called it.

Each evening as I sat with Hob, I imagined him surrounded by light. He seemed to be in a deeply peaceful state. Yet I wondered how, silent and alone, he had adjusted to the irreversible effects of the stroke. Given the depth of how he had reflected on the subject of death, where was he in the process of letting go into things as they were, into the immanence of his own death? No answers to these questions. Only the invitation to trust something beyond what was apparent.

I stayed with the images of light. I imagined that the light around him extended to fill the room, then radiated out beyond the room, into the neighborhood, into the city, into the larger world. I imagined it as best I could, because it invited a deep calm and helped to expand the particulars of our situation into something vast, inclusive, and loving.

By now, about five weeks after his stroke, there was another shift, subtle but significant: Hob had begun to refuse food. At first his refusals were sporadic. He'd refuse one meal but then eat again for the next several meals. It seemed obvious that all we could do was to follow his lead. Along with eating less, he was clearly in deeper, longer periods of sleep.

One evening as I sat there, I suddenly knew that the time had come to begin letting him go. It was a clear realization, a knowing. I leaned over him, laid my cheek against his for a moment, and told him that I was going to do a guided meditation with him. I gazed for a moment at his right hand, at his long, tapered fingers that curled slightly on the light blue blanket that covered him. I saw the familiar patterning of his veins and the sun-mottled variations of his skin. I didn't reach toward him to lay my hand on top of his as I usually would have done. For these moments anyway, our only connection would be the sound of my voice as I recited the Clear Light meditation[1], a simple yet profound guided visualization from the Tibetan tradition to recite with the dying, a practice in which I had trained many years earlier.

I began to watch the rise and fall of Hob's breathing. His breath would be my focus for the duration of the meditation.

As I settled into stillness, I felt the unsurpassable tenderness of the moment. For, however attuned I may have been to his state, the decision to start the visualization was a conscious act of letting him go. It was an acknowledgment that the end was near.

Feeling the rhythms of his out-breaths, I attuned my breathing to the rhythm of his. In a steady, soothing voice, with each of his out-breaths, I began to recite the phrases, allowing pauses between each one.

Visualize a vast, boundless ocean of light . . .

There is light everywhere . . . clear, radiant light . . .

There is light above . . . there is light below . . .

There is light to the right . . . light to the left . . .

There is light within . . . there is light without . . .

Light everywhere . . . a vast, radiant ocean of light . . .

Letting go into light . . .

Breathing into light . . . following breath into light . . .

Becoming one with light . . .

Merging with light . . . a clear, radiant ocean of light . . .

I continued for a while longer with variations of the phrases, then sat in silence. The reverberations of the phrases continued within. An invitation to keep letting go. To just be. All thoughts silenced. Only being present with each breath, the flickering light, and the sense that all was well.

<hr>

For the next several evenings, I did the Clear Light visualization with Hob. As I recited the phrases, their meaning would wash over me, ease my fatigue, and leave me deep in serenity. Beyond the words, I sensed the deep connection between us. It was the sixth night since I'd started the guided meditation with him. I climbed the stairs to my room and fell into an unusually deep sleep.

A few hours later, violently startled, I was lifted, heart pounding, out of a heavy sleep. In a flash of awareness, I realized that someone was standing by my bed. I knew it even before I opened my eyes. I felt only the thundering in my chest, an urgent drumbeat announcing that something was out of the ordinary.

I'm pulling myself up from the depths of sleep. . . . Heart pounding. . . . Something very strange happening here, initially frightening. . . . Suddenly dramatically awake. . . . Staring hard into the darkened room. . . . Straining to see the form between bed and bureau. . . . It seems suspended in space. . . . Very still . . . overwhelmingly strong. . . . The form darker than the surrounding room . . . . Yet benevolent, not dark as in threatening. . . . A silent, intense presence watching me, watching over me. . . . Roaring silence but no impulse to speak. . . . A powerful meeting of two energy fields . . . . Together . . . yet separate. . . . Now beginning to dissolve. . . . Still I look, staring into the dissolving form. . . . Trying to sustain contact. . . . But it dissolves . . . the form into the formless . . . leaving only roaring silence. . . . And this pounding heart, slowly quieting. . . .

I was alone again in the room. Then the questions: who had come to stand beside the bed? I had no reference point for this experience. Was it Hob? In recent days he often seemed beyond deep sleep, in other states of consciousness. I assumed that this was part of the natural evolution toward death, where he was getting ready to leave, where he might already be free of the body at times.

Was this a portent of his death? I knew it wasn't a dream because I was fully, dramatically awake. The reality of the last few days had already been both ordinary and awesome. Ordinary because the details of caregiving continued as life moved along with its daily demands. Ordinary because at one level, death is just that: ordinary. Awesome because the imminence of death is just that.

The following morning Hob was in a still deeper, more distant state. That afternoon the hospice nurse confirmed that he had slipped into a coma. Except for the occasional groans when we needed to care for his body, the rest of the time he seemed to be in a state of deep peace, lying there with the fall sunlight spilling into the room, brightening everything.

The following night, I had a powerful dream.

I am climbing alone in a mountainous area, clambering up treacherous inclines toward a summit I cannot see. I pull myself onto a rock outcropping where I stop to rest and look at the view. From here I see two striking images. To my left, a stream cascades down to a large pool which is below me to the right. The pool is deep and translucent; the surface of the pool is very still. There is one large saffron and gold fish with white markings swimming in the pool. It is striking because its markings are those of a tropical fish, not a trout or some other freshwater fish.

Then I look up toward the left and see a flock of birds as they veer suddenly and fly toward where I am standing. I marvel at them because the birds, about twenty in number, are of all different varieties, brilliant blues, greens, reds, and oranges—different colors in resplendent combinations.

I almost lose my balance on the high rock because I am so entranced by these sights. Only then do I realize how dangerous it is up here, and I am alone. Who would help if I were to fall, be seriously hurt, or killed?

I awoke, startled by the energy of the dream, its images charged with symbolism: the translucent pool, the saffron-colored fish, the variegated flock of birds. Then came the associations, rich with symbolic meaning from Hob's life: his passion for streams and for searching out the hidden pools where the trout might lie. The symbol of the fish, *ichthys*, secretly drawn on the ground in early Christian days to identify oneself as a fellow Christian. The color saffron had particular significance; it was Hob's favorite color, the one he had loved above all others. In many traditions, birds are seen as messengers of spirit, intermediaries between earth and air, between the visible and the invisible. Birds frequently appear in association with death. In the dream, to me they symbolized Hob's rich inner life: his love of literature and passion for music, his explorations of consciousness and dedication to the meditative path, his openness to the wisdom traditions that had graced his life. The dream images, as vivid as waking reality, accompanied me through the coming days.

It was the day before Thanksgiving, a clear, cold day with a brisk wind. In a wild dance, the late fall leaves raced across the lawn, settled into sheltered corners under the bushes, and blew up against the sliding glass doors just beyond where Hob's bed stood. That morning his breathing changed into rapid, shallow breaths.

I sat by his bed and coordinated my breathing with this new rhythm. I noticed how the rhythm was punctuated by an occasional deeper breath and a gentle groan. Neither Jocylyne nor I sensed that he was in pain. Rather this was the sound of effort, as if he were trying to get free. He was definitely working now, his body in a new stage where yet another involuntary system had taken over.

The room was charged with a new energy. As I sat with him, I felt the imminence of death, simple and natural, mysterious and awesome.

Jocylyne and I conferred about his state quietly in the next room. She encouraged me to go ahead with my plans for the day. She reminded me that this pattern could go on for several days.

I was headed for Grandparents' Day at our grandson's school. It was the day before the Thanksgiving holiday, and the school was electric with the excitement of children, heightened by visiting family and the prospect of days off from school. I tried to be present, but I was living in two realities. I picked up some blocks and began to build a structure with my grandson and his friends, but I kept feeling Hob's breathing pulling at my attention. I moved, dreamlike, through special moments with four-year-olds, conversations with grandparents, and the school assembly.

**Life and death upon one tether
And running beautiful together.**[2]

Hob's quotation came back to me that morning.

The day passed more slowly than usual. The rapid breathing continued into the afternoon and evening when Ethan came by to sit with Hob for a few minutes.

"Hi Dad, it's Ethan. I'm here." He reached out and touched his father's hand, which lay across his chest. He sat quietly for a short while, then came out of the living room. His face was etched in pain.

"It makes me uncomfortable to see Dad breathing like that."

"I know. It's hard for me, too. It seems he's working pretty hard now. There's nothing we can do except be with him. And keep him comfortable."

"Well, let me know if anything changes."

Conversations were short and perfunctory now, words hollow, inadequate. I returned to the living room and sat, again synchronizing my breathing with Hob's. "Tomorrow is

Thanksgiving, Hobbie. I'll be here except for when I go to have dinner with the family in the late afternoon."

For some reason, I felt it was important to tell him my plans. When I spoke those words, I remembered the Native American expression, "Today is a good day to die, when all the things of life are in order." This was the attitude with which they lived. Greet each day as a gift, yet also accept that death can occur at any time. Indeed, I thought, Thanksgiving would be a good day to die.

Over the weeks, we'd evolved an evening ritual for the end of the day. I say *we* intentionally. In those seven weeks, Hob and I had spent a lot of time together in silence. I could talk with him and sense not only his listening but sometimes his response, the sense that we were in communication beyond words. These silent conversations were as vivid to me as any spoken ones we'd ever had.

That evening I sat by his bed, my hand covering his, and told him how gracefully he'd lived this last chapter of his life, that he'd been an inspiration to friends who saw that it was possible to bring humor and lightness to difficult circumstances. It was a great gift, his final and most profound teaching.

Sensing how important it was to affirm his life even as he was dying, I reminded him:

That he had led a courageous and compassionate life.

That he had touched the lives of countless people.

That he'd been a wonderful teacher, a loyal friend, a devoted father, and that included our struggles as a family.

That he'd been a real adventurer of the spirit, always taking the leap into the next exploration of consciousness; how I loved that about him and was immensely grateful that he'd led me into places I might not have gone without him. And the other way around.

That he'd been unfailingly dedicated to understanding the causes of suffering, and had helped alleviate the sufferings of so many people.

How our journey together, though far from smooth at times, had been a great trip.

How I appreciated beyond words the great depth of our relationship and how it had unfolded over the years.

How, although we couldn't know, I still imagined that the presence of the wise ones was here at this time: Father Bede, Thay (Thich Nhat Hanh), Lise, Anandamayi Ma, Ramana Maharshi, and the others who'd been sources of inspiration for him.

How, even though I would miss him enormously, I prayed that his leaving—the ultimate freedom—would be gentle and happen soon.

How, even though he was leaving, I felt boundless gratitude for our lives together.

That I simply loved to be with him.

Sensing that all had been said, I asked him if he could feel the tremendous love surrounding us.

His breathing filled the space with its strong, urgent rhythm, but he looked serene. I noticed how long his silver hair had grown over the weeks, a wavy mane that rested against the pillow. The November wind raced through the trees outside, magnifying the sense of being suspended in a safe cocoon where an invisible process quietly continued.

I moved into the ritual that had become the way each day ended. I began by chanting the three refuges in honor of his Buddhist roots.

Buddham sharinam gacchami "I take refuge in the Buddha."
Dharmam sharinam gacchami "I take refuge in the dharma."
Sangham sharinam gacchami "I take refuge in the sangha."

The second chant came from the tradition of the Indian saint Ramana Maharshi. It celebrated a form of the divine. Then I softly sang a favorite chant from Taizé, the ecumenical Christian monastery in France. *Ubi caritas et amor, ubi caritas, deus ibi est.* "Wherever loving-kindness is, God is there." Its gentle, simple melody sounded like a lullaby that night.

Then, finally, another Buddhist chant that we sometimes sang before meditation: *Gate gate paragate parasamgate bodhi swaha!* The words point to the state of unitary consciousness. "Gone, gone beyond, gone even beyond, so be it!" As I sang, I absorbed the meaning of these ancient words, loving the beauty of the Sanskrit, feeling assured that at this level, all was indeed well.

I rose, leaned over, and kissed Hob goodnight. I knew in that moment, as I had known so many times before, that this might be the last time.

Deep in the night, I awoke suddenly from a heavy sleep and felt a flicker of annoyance that something had interrupted my much-needed rest. A few moments later, the light went on in the hall. I knew instantly that Jocylyne was coming to get me. We had an agreement that if anything changed in Hob's condition, she would wake me. I jumped out of bed, opened the door, and saw her standing halfway up the stairs.

"He just left," she said matter-of-factly, her eyes luminous with tears. "It was very easy. He just went out on one of those heavier breaths."

A deep calm accompanied me down the stairs and into the living room. There he lay, looking exactly as I had left him a few hours earlier, except now there was an immense stillness. His body was as warm as ever, as if nothing at all had changed. He looked strikingly beautiful, even noble, in death; the lifelines on his face had all but disappeared. A sense of deep peace surrounded him.

I glanced at my watch. It was a few minutes after midnight of Thanksgiving day. Yes, Thanksgiving, a good day to die. I lit the candle on the altar and sat down in the chair beside his bed. Quiet, expectant, I tried to tune in to what might be happening for him. I could sense the growing distance. Yet it also felt as if the room was filled with a very strong presence, ineffable, inexplicable, but unmistakably there. At that point, I had no feelings of distress or loss. Only feelings of relief and gratitude that he was free. And my sense of a boundless, peaceful presence.

In those moments, death seemed so easy and simple.

According to Buddhist teachings, hearing is the last of the senses to go and, it is believed, continues even after physical death. I began to talk quietly. First to tell him that this was the transition known as death, and then to resume the quiet, inspiring phrases of the guided meditation. Never before had the phrases of the visualization been so charged with significance and energy. I moved into an expanded, timeless state, and sat there for half an hour.

I would have remained in the experience longer except that we wanted to care for Hob's body ourselves. We needed to do that soon. I went to the phone and called Ethan who arrived about fifteen minutes later.

I wished that Laura could be with us to participate in caring for her father in death, but she'd gone to her husband's family for Thanksgiving. So the three of us, Ethan, Jocylyne, and I, moved seamlessly into working together. A few words here and there, even laughter as we struggled to dress Hob. Finally we put on his body the brown jacket that he had received at his ordination, the signature of the Vietnamese order of monks, the Tiep Hien Order, and symbolic of the simple cotton clothes worn by Vietnamese peasants.

This jacket represented the most significant arc of Hob's life journey, one which had started with the conservative, privileged childhood of an American boy from the Midwest, who ended up in death wearing not a suit but a simple peasant's jacket from a country halfway around the world.

There was something comforting and ritualistic about all the details of Hob's final care. I was especially heartened that Ethan was part of the ancient ritual of those closest to the deceased caring for their dead. Once again, he was the son who moved willingly into an unfamiliar role, caring for his father in unfamiliar circumstances, work traditionally done by women or by strangers.

We then set about to transform the room. We removed all the signs of hospice care. We brought additional flowers from the planting window. And on the little table beside where Hob lay, I set up another altar with a candle, a small flowering plant, the little Buddha that the Dalai Lama had given him after their interview, and the two packets from T.T. A sense of order and deep peace pervaded the room. This was the way everything would remain for the next three days while family members and friends came to sit with Hob, endings and beginnings all woven into a seamless web.

CONCERNING DEATH AND DYING
Reflections

* Hob had told me that mental loss was all about "getting down to speed." His words truly hit the mark. For caregivers, the challenge is to slow down and align one's rhythms with the patient.

* In the acute phase of terminal illness and with the

immanence of death, our sense of life may become vividly focused. The sheer force of circumstances rivets our attention to all the details: moment by moment we need to respond to the patient's needs. At the same time, there is the possibility of holding a spacious perspective, one that reminds us of the countless others also keeping vigil; that this final stage of life can deepen us in ways we couldn't have imagined; that healing of relationships is possible right up until death and beyond; that death is the most powerful of teachers.

* Although every situation is unique, I was acutely aware of two realities: first, the daily demands of care, and secondly, Hob's inner process. I could only intuit the latter. The question is when to reach out to provide connection (touching, talking quietly, playing music, etc.) and when to leave the patient to uninterrupted experiencing? Finding this balance involves both sensitivity and intuition.

* In the final stages, one is simultaneously immersed in the demands of care and faced with the enormity of what's happening. At this time, it's easy to feel isolated—a hallmark of illness whether for the patient or for caregivers. Again, it may be helpful to remember that the personal and universal are interwoven, that we are engaged in the universal ritual of moving toward death, that we are not alone even though what we are

experiencing feels totally unique and personal.

* Sometimes I wondered how it was possible to feel, even in the midst of difficult circumstances, that *at some level all was well.* The emphasis here is on the word *level.* The wisdom traditions speak about the relative and absolute levels of reality. Relative reality is the world as we know it—conditioned, governed by duality—whereas absolute reality is unconditioned, beyond duality, free. We can have glimpses of that level even in the presence of death.

Suggestions

* When under duress, it's easy to forget the simplest things that might help. Review Khandro Rinpoche's short statements from our meeting (chapter 10). For me, they were wise reminders for getting through the most intense of life experiences—by-standing Hob's passage into death while simultaneously letting him go. The most valuable ones for me were "Be easy with yourself," "The best practice is calm abiding," and "Go beyond hope and fear."

* Recognizing how Hob lived in a world of accelerating loss, I wanted to affirm the goodness of his life for him, to remind him of the many ways in which he had touched the lives of others. Whoever we are, however humble or hidden our lives, we have left our gifts, from the smallest acts of kindness to highly visible contributions. I found it moving to recall some of those gifts for Hob now that he was so deeply impaired.

* It is difficult for some people to be comfortable with the silence that surrounds one who is close to death. Often the simplest things are the best. Coordinate the rhythm of your breathing with theirs. (If their breathing is labored or erratic, let your breathing be steady and calm.) Repeat silently to yourself (or in a soft voice) a few sacred words, a short prayer, or a mantra. Feel that you are surrounding the patient with peace, blessings, light, or whatever feels right to you. The gift of a calm, loving presence is immeasurable.

* Reread the five seed thoughts from Tulku Thondup (see page 250-251). See how they might apply to your situation and adapt them so they work for you. I found the image of blessing light particularly comforting and inspiring. The nature of that light is calming and peaceful, something I invoked for myself, then for Hob, then for all beings, visualizing that light moving out in ever-widening circles as far as imagination could extend it.

Seed Thoughts

May I be calm and peaceful.

Give me strength and equanimity.

POSTLUDE

"DANCE ME TO THE END OF LOVE"

After Hob's death, the days were filled with the flurry of activity that such times demand—notifying family and friends, receiving visitors, arranging the memorial service. Grief wrapped me in a finely woven cocoon to protect me from the enormity of loss. Of course life went on, yet I felt dislocated. Then someone's words or a memory would penetrate the cocoon, and the full force of my feelings overflowed—painful but life-giving—and I'd feel reconnected to the world around me.

I sensed that grief took a different course for those who lost a loved one to Alzheimer's or some other form of brain disease. Faced with the continuous losses that the disease perpetrates, we grieve the losses as we go along. By the time death finally comes, we've already done a lot of grieving. When Hob died, I had already gone through many cycles of grief. Yet still, the finality, the end of almost forty years of relationship, left me feeling abandoned in an unfamiliar element, as if I were trying to walk underwater.

I continued to mine the depths of what he and I had been through together, to search for meaning in the losses, to affirm what had been positive. For example, a few days after his death, while in conversation with a friend, I remembered one of the most arresting statements Hob ever made about his illness.

"This Alzheimer's is the best f***ing education I've ever had," he had said, both exasperated and chuckling as he wrestled with how to convey something to me. As someone who practically never swore, his use of the "f" word gave inordinate meaning to his message. He had had a lifelong interest in the nature of the mind, and naturally he would be intrigued—as well as fearful and dismayed—to watch what was happening to his own mind.

He had been fortunate: he had died more or less in the late middle stages of the illness, and some measure of awareness had stayed with him throughout, albeit increasingly fragmented in the last couple of years. Anyone steeped in meditation has had a lot of experience with acceptance and letting go. These are invaluable assets as we move into the later years and toward death. As the Sufi saying goes, "Die before you die, and you won't die when you die."

This statement refers to the death of the ego—the sense of a separate core identity that we protect and defend at great cost. In the course of his illness, Hob experienced countless ego deaths. The most monumental one occurred that night at the meditation center when his carefully prepared talk dissolved into fragments.

How can one tolerate a dissolving world with any measure of ease? Hob wasn't always able to; on occasion he became flustered, frustrated, and fearful. But much of the time, he was blessed with the gift of seeing the humor of his own dilemmas, which lightened things up for him and everyone around him.

One morning about ten days before he died, Emily, a great-hearted Brazilian woman who came periodically to help with housecleaning, walked into the living room to visit Hob. She greeted him warmly.

"How are you doing this morning?" It was a pleasantry that didn't need or expect a reply. Then she leaned closer over the bed, took hold of his hand, and with a lilt in her voice, she said:

"The most important thing is to be happy!"

That was hardly an ordinary comment to someone who was dying, but from Emily, it sounded uplifting and totally natural. As the faintest hint of a smile flickered across Hob's face, he answered in his best Indian accent, one he loved for its musical cadences, including their idiomatic way of adding the word *only* for emphasis.

"Be happy only," Hob said in his enfeebled voice.

She laughed as she leaned forward to hug him, bringing their exchange to an end.

Unwittingly—or perhaps not—she had struck the most resonant chord. More than almost any teaching, Hob had embraced this very one about finding happiness in the present moment—a statement that is preposterously obvious, deceptively simple, but not always so easily lived out.

Those were the last words I heard him speak. How fitting—words that could be heard as a universal wish for all beings, everywhere.

As I looked back over the six years, I saw some of the phases that had been part of our journey. How in the early years I sometimes felt burdened by the responsibility of companioning Hob on this journey. How, gradually, a deep level of acceptance replaced my struggles and doubts. How committed both of us were to live the years as consciously and lovingly as possible. How there had been cycles—of discouragement, fatigue, determination—and then acceptance where all was well with the world in spite of the challenges. How I became determined to accompany him wholeheartedly, because both of us knew that along with the most difficult, harrowing times, there would also be lessons, some hidden treasures.

We had appreciated the unexpected gifts: the understanding that we'd made an agreement at the soul level to do this together—a karmic bond that gave a deeper meaning to the illness; Hob's humor and curiosity about what was happening to his mind; the loving support of family and friends, particularly the family group and the memorable meeting with Jim and Louise to address Hob's preoccupation with death; the suggestion that *how* he lived with the illness was his new form of teaching. We found inspiration in seemingly small phrases such as "the grace of diminishment" or "the majesty of your loving," which I would invoke to help us remember the bits of wisdom that could lighten our load. For above all, the greatest gift came from feeling everyone's love around us, as well as that which flowered between us.

On Christmas morning three years after his diagnosis, much to my surprise Hob had handed me a present. That year he was already a long way from remembering—much less buying—a Christmas present. I took the carefully wrapped package, surely the work of our daughter Laura's hands, and sat down on the couch in our Vermont living room, Hob on my right, our son Ethan on my left, Laura in the rocking chair. Inside the wrappings appeared a large slender book with a striking cover. Five naked women held hands in a circle as they danced with carefree abandon against an abstract background of dark blue and green. I recognized the reproduction of "The Dancers," one of Henri Matisse's most famous paintings. Above the painting appeared the title of the book: "Dance Me to the End of Love," the title of a poem by Leonard Cohen.

I opened the book. There on the bright red frontispiece, the inscription read, "Merry Christmas for Olivia dear . . . 'Dance me to the end of love 'till I'm safely gathered in . . .' Ever, H." Under his initial he had drawn two hearts with an arrow joining them. I felt the tears rising. I couldn't imagine how he had ever managed to get this book, much less write these touching words in his now unsteady hand.

"Mom, I saw the book in Seattle and decided to buy it for Dad to give you," said Laura, her own eyes teary. "It's actually a song by Leonard Cohen, and the book combines a series of Matisse paintings to illustrate each line of his tribute to love. Why don't you let Dad read a couple of the lines."

I handed the book to him and he began to read.

"This first line is the one that really gets me," Hob said.

Dance me through the panic 'til I'm gathered safely in
Lift me like an olive branch and be my homeward dove
Dance me to the end of love. . . .
Dance me very tenderly and dance me very long
We're both of us beneath our love, we're both of us above
Dance me to the end of love.[1]

Hob looked up, his eyes now filled with tears, too. The four of us each recognized the gift of the poem's prophetic words.

For the next three years, that Christmas book migrated back and forth from the living room to the family room. *Dance me to the end of love until I'm safely gathered in*—those lines reminded us of the greater journey on which we were embarked. The words were an inspiration and a balm at the same time.

In the days and weeks following Hob's death, reminiscences floated spontaneously into my mind—memories, dreams, or symbolic markers that had special significance. I was revisited by the healing image of the dolphin that had leapt into my lap and the wheeling birds of the last big dream before his death. Both of us had tracked the slow demise of the great maple—our old friend at the top of the meadow in Vermont. Each year we had wondered whether it would survive another harsh Vermont winter. It died that year—the same year that Hob died. He never knew how I had watched the dying back of the tree, a symbol that for me paralleled Hob's own decline.

In retrospect, I even felt uplifted at remembering some of the treacherous territory we had negotiated together: his perplexities and fears, the medical emergencies, the reality of living for so long with the imminence of death. The presence of death gave our lives immediacy. We treasured the little moments: the sunlight flooding into the family room on a spring morning, the liquid song of the cardinal in the elm outside the window, the touch of hands as we reached for closeness even as his illness moved us toward separation. The deep connection was always there.

I even found ways to accept and listen to his stories. Repeated as many times as they were, listening to his repetitive fragments of conversation became a practice; I cultivated patience and tried to hear his words as if for the first time. Certainly I experienced plenty of boredom and frustration. Yet frequently I would feel a surge of love and compassion for him, realizing the enormity of what he was dealing with—this person I loved who once himself had spoken "with the tongues of angels," a phrase he savored and used for people whose gift of speaking he admired.

Naturally, I wondered how I would have handled the challenges he was dealing with. Would I have had his patience, his sense of humor? Would I have been able to find ways to keep sharing my gifts with others, in spite of serious verbal impairment? He had lived through those years with extraordinary courage, nobility, and humor. Sometimes I felt as if my heart was breaking open with the power of my feelings for him. I understood that the people around us couldn't know how, along with the grief and challenges, unseen blessings were woven through the complexities. And the greatest of these was the love. It kept deepening with the adversity.

We had gone through an initiation, as great an initiation

as life can offer two people. Was this my rationalization? No. I came to accept the truth of this perspective. As we were held in the fire of transformation, we were burned and burnished until the gold of love shone unobstructed between us. That was, ultimately, the blessing and the gift of the journey.

APPENDIX ONE
CLEAR LIGHT MEDITATION

A Guided Meditation for the Dying

Many years before my husband's illness, I had trained in meditation practices for the dying. These practices, universal in nature, are based on the premise that the moment of death is a time of profound spiritual opportunity. It is then that the clear light dawns in the mind, a boundless luminosity that signifies the transition from life to death. Simple guided meditations can help the dying one to open and remain in this clear light.

The Clear Light Society, an organization founded by Patricia Shelton in the late 1970s, trains people in meditations that offer gentle guidance at the time of death. Although the basic Clear Light meditation comes from the Tibetan tradition, images of light associated with death are universal in nature. The Tibetans have perhaps the most extensive knowledge about the states of consciousness experienced at death and beyond. The Clear Light practice has been called a "Mind Treasure" suitable for our times, and the guiding phrases can be used with anyone, whether they are spiritually inclined or not. Nonsectarian in nature, this meditation prepares the mind of the dying person for the transition of death.

Speaking personally, I have been very grateful for these meditations when present with someone who is dying, whether my husband, my mother, friends, or the hospice patients and their families (only when it felt appropriate) with whom I was privileged to work. First of all, there is perhaps nothing more helpful than to offer a calm presence leading up to the time of death, to sit quietly while coordinating one's breathing with the patient. This has been called co-meditation, a way of being with a loved one who is approaching death. Here are some simple guidelines.

The rising and falling of the breath becomes your meditative focus. Synchronize your breathing with theirs. If their breath is very short, labored, or irregular, you can try breathing in slow, calm breaths instead. Tell them quietly that you are breathing along with them and that you will be giving them some simple suggestions that help to relax and let go—or whatever words feel appropriate to you.

Traditionally, it is preferable not to touch the person while doing this meditation, the purpose being to help them let go into freedom and spaciousness. This is, however, a deeply personal matter where one needs to follow one's intuition about what feels right.

Begin by helping them to relax by repeating three to five (or more) sounds of *ahhh* . . . with their out-breaths. *Ahh* is the sound of letting go, of releasing and easing into whatever is happening. Making sound can be particularly helpful if there is discomfort or pain. Let your sound of *ahh* be gentle but firm, sounding it the whole length of their out-breath, and trusting that even this simple practice is helpful for someone in this heightened, subtle state.

GUIDELINES FOR THE GUIDED MEDITATION

What follows are a series of simple phrases to repeat quietly on the out-breath. Sometimes you may be able to say only one word or part of a phrase. One goes very slowly, feeling free to pause for a breath or two, so there is no sense of hurry. This is a visualization on opening to the light—the "ground luminosity"—a common experience of near-death experiencers and people who have intuited these states in deep meditation. The version below is a universal form.

Explain to the person that you'll be repeating some phrases that all have to do with visualizing light. Since it takes time to enter the imagery, take plenty of time, repeating the phrases or making up your own. You'll find the phrases help you to focus and relax as well as helping the patient, especially if the circumstances are difficult (their pain, hospital rooms, labored breathing, etc.). Cultivate steadiness. We're trying to convey a state of peace and acceptance no matter what is happening.

Ahh . . . ahh . . . ahh . . .
Visualize a vast, boundless ocean of light . . .
There is light everywhere . . . clear, radiant light . . .
There is light above . . . there is light below . . .

There is light to the right . . . there is light to the left . . .

There is light within . . . there is light without . . .

Light everywhere . . . a vast, radiant ocean of light . . .

Letting go into the light . . .

Breathing into the light . . .

Following breath into light . . .

Trusting the light . . .

Becoming one with the light . . .

Flowing into light . . .

Letting go into light . . .

Merging with the light . . . a clear, radiant ocean of light . . .

There is only light . . .

Becoming one with light . . .

Breathing light into light . . .

Everywhere light . . .

Light . . . light . . . boundless, radiant light . . . etc.

ANOTHER PRACTICE

One can also repeat the following phrases, again speaking quietly on each out-breath.

Quiet mind . . . peaceful heart . . .

Quiet mind . . . peaceful heart . . .

Repeat these two phrases as often as feels right, allowing

the space of a breath or two between phrases. One can do this anytime to help the person relax and let go as you offer them your caring presence.

For further information and training, log on to www.clearlightsociety.org.

APPENDIX TWO

CARING FOR LOVED ONES IN DEATH

In recent years, there has been a growing movement to reclaim how we care for our loved ones in death. In the same way that hospice care has allowed people to die at home, similarly we can do far more than we may realize to reclaim all aspects of what happens at death.

So thoroughly has the funeral business appropriated care of the deceased, many people have no idea of their options. While acknowledging the variations among different religious traditions, it can be deeply rewarding to honor death as a spiritual passage and create rituals that are meaningful to you. Many people may still prefer to let the funeral business take over, but for those who are uncomfortable with the ways and costs of funeral directors, the purpose of this section is to empower families to reclaim the freedom to care for the deceased in their own ways.

Throughout time, humankind has evolved rituals for dealing with the significant passages of life. These rituals always contain practical, physical elements as well as symbolic, spiritual ones. Caring for the body in death is one of these rituals. It is a deeply moving and natural process. It helps to complete the process of letting go and accepting the reality of the death. If we keep the deceased at home for a day or more, it allows family and friends the opportunity to say goodbye, grieve, and more easily let go in a familiar, more comfortable setting. We may have spent days, months, or longer caring for this person; taking care of the body in death completes this circle of caring.

Here are some of the important facts that you should know.

* You can serve as your own funeral director, handling many, if not all, of the functions of the funeral business. The laws vary by state.

* You should know that the cost of a conventional funeral, with body burial, can exceed $10,000.

* Although laws vary between states, you can keep the deceased at home for one to three days. Bodies do not decompose right away and embalming is not required. In hot weather, the body can be kept cool with dry ice. Nothing is needed in cool weather.

* You can fill out all the necessary forms yourself.

* You can build your own coffin, buy an alternative cremation container inexpensively from a local crematory, or have a funeral director deliver your choice of container to your home.

* In many states, you can transport the body in your own vehicle.

* You can wash, shave, anoint, dress, and create a sacred space around the body with flowers, candles, and meaningful objects.

* You can choose which professional services of a funeral director you want to use, rather than buying the standard package.

* There are more than 150 memorial societies, now called Funeral Consumer Alliances, in the United States and Canada to help families plan simple, dignified, meaningful, and affordable arrangements for the deceased. Information is available on the website www.funerals.org. This site accesses the national organization, from which there are links to local affiliates in specific states with more detailed information and contacts for your area.

* Helpful and sensitive professional advice is available by phone on caring for the body, burial/cremation arrangements, legal requirements, and information on reasonably priced and ecological caskets.

* All of these arrangements should be researched before the time of death so the family is prepared.

APPENDIX THREE
TOPICS FOR DISCUSSION

The Boston Alzheimer's Center, which Hob attended, helped the participants to continue sharing what they loved, even with their impairments, for as long as others seemed to enjoy it. Since teaching meditation had been central to Hob's life, the staff encouraged him to keep teaching as long as he could, offering their support in running the group. Each week I helped him choose some words of wisdom for discussion before he'd lead a simple guided meditation. Since the topics for discussion turned out to be rewarding for both Hob and the staff, I've included quotations that can be used in courses, support groups, or any other setting that deals with issues of aging.

For easy reference, I've divided the quotations into categories, some of which naturally overlap. Some of the quotes stand alone, whereas others include questions for discussion.

THE OPPORTUNITIES OF AGING

1. In my younger years, I thanked God for this expanding, growing life. In my later years, when I found my physical powers

growing less, I thanked God also for what I called the grace of diminishment.

— Teilhard de Chardin, French philosopher, priest, mystic

2. Because my memory has been affected, I'm no longer bound to past and future in the same way, and the relief of this is enormous. For this reason, illness and aging contain the seeds of great opportunity in terms of spiritual growth.

— Ram Dass, in *Still Here: Embracing Aging, Changing, and Dying*

Discussion

What are some of the seeds of opportunity in our lives right now?

What about the joys of living in the present moment (versus regrets about the past or worries about the future)?

3. It's very simple. As you grow older, you learn more. Aging is not just decay, you know. It's growth. It's more than the negative that you're going to die; it's also the positive that you *understand* you're going to die, and that you live a better life because of it.

— Morrie Schwartz, in *Tuesdays with Morrie*, by Mitch Albom

Discussion

In what ways are we growing in this process of growing older?

4. If you can come to see aging not as the demise of your body but the harvest of your soul, you will learn that aging can be a time of great strength . . . and confidence.

— John O'Donohue, in *Anam Cara (Anam cara* means "spiritual friend.")

Discussion

When do we feel confident and in touch with our strengths?

What are the situations that challenge our confidence?

5. Aging can be a lovely time of ripening when you actually meet yourself, indeed maybe for the first time. There are beautiful lines from T.S. Eliot that say:

> And the end of all our exploring
> Will be to arrive where we started
> And to know the place for the first time.

— John O'Donohue, in *Anam Cara*

6. One of the joys of aging is that you have more time to be still. . . . Stillness is vital to the world of the soul. If as you age you become more still, you discover that stillness can be a great companion.

— John O'Donohue, in *Anam Cara*

THE PRESENT MOMENT

7. Our appointment with life is in the present moment.

— Thich Nhat Hanh, meditation teacher, writer, peace activist, in *Our Appointment with Life: Buddha's Teaching on Living in the Present*

8. It's interesting how little of the past is required to have a present moment.

— Ram Dass, in *Still Here: Embracing Aging, Changing, and Dying*

9. By making stillness necessary, it slows us down to the present moment. Although I would like my memory back, I recognize the advantages of memory loss and use it to fully enter the present.
— Ram Dass, in *Still Here: Embracing Aging, Changing, and Dying*

10. If we cannot come home to ourselves in the present moment, we cannot be in touch with life. When we are in touch with the peaceful and healing elements within ourselves, and around us, we learn how to cherish and protect these things and make them grow. These elements of peace are available to us any time.
— Thich Nhat Hanh, in *Peace Is Every Step: The Path of Mindfulness in Everyday Life*

Discussion

What are the peaceful and healing elements in our lives right now?

What are some of the challenges that keep us from feeling peaceful?

11. Practice (or living wisely) is learning to cherish the well-being that is already here.
— Thich Nhat Hanh

12. Time and again, we miss out on the great treasures in our lives because we are so restless. In our minds we are always elsewhere. We are seldom in the place where we stand and in the time that is now.
— John O'Donohue, in *Anam Cara*

Soul/Spirit

13. The good news is that the spirit is more powerful than the vicissitudes of aging. . . . I can say to you now that faith and love are stronger than any changes, stronger than aging, and, I am very sure, stronger than death.

— Ram Dass, in *Still Here: Embracing Aging, Changing, and Dying*

Discussion

When do we feel the presence of spirit in our lives, and when do we feel tested and out of touch with it?

In what ways might we cultivate a deeper relationship with spirit in our lives?

14. Your mind can be possessed of illusions, but your spirit is eternally free.

— *A Course in Miracles*

15. Aging is not merely about the body losing its poise, strength, and self-trust. Aging also invites you to become aware of the sacred circle that shelters your life.

— John O'Donohue, in *Anam Cara*

Discussion

Who and what make you feel safe and sheltered in your life?

Have you ever thought about the "sacred circle" of your life, and the people, places, and activities that contribute to that circle?

⸺ ᥴ∞ᥩ ⸺

Fear and Worry

16. Fear is not of the present, but only of the past and future, which do not exist in this moment.

— *A Course in Miracles*

Discussion

What helps us when we start worrying or feeling afraid?

Do you have some saying or prayer that can help you?

Or some family member or friend you could turn to?

17. My life has taught me to be more curious than afraid.

— Ishi, Native American elder, in Pema Chödrön's *Start Where You Are: A Guide to Compassionate Living*

18. Fear creates the abyss. Love crosses it.

— Sri Nisargadatta Maharaj, Indian teacher, in *I Am That, Talks with Sri Nisargadatta Maharaj*

Discussion

How might we bring more curiosity and acceptance to the process of aging and loss?

Who makes us feel loved, and do we tell them how much they mean to us?

CULTIVATING POSITIVE QUALITIES

19. My religion is kindness. . . . The important thing is to have a good heart, a warm heart in daily life. This is the principle of life.
— H. H. the Dalai Lama

20. I believe that the very purpose of our life is to seek happiness. Whether one believes in religion or not, we are all seeking something better in life. So, I think, the very motion of our life is towards happiness.
— H. H. the Dalai Lama, in *The Art of Happiness: A Handbook for Living*

21. Perhaps joy is one of God's commandments.
— Rachel Remen, in *My Grandfather's Blessings*

Discussion

How can we be in touch with the seeds of joy in our lives, even as we learn to accept our challenges?

Think about the things that bring you joy in your life, remembering the small ones that we sometimes overlook.

22. Some people can be very compassionate to others but are exceptionally harsh with themselves. One of the qualities that you develop, particularly in your older years, is a sense of great compassion toward yourself.
— John O'Donohue, in *Anam Cara*

NOTES

CHAPTER 1

1. Based on John Milton's "On His Deceased Wife." For the complete poem, see *The Oxford Book of English Verse: 1250-1900*, also available online at Bartleby.com.

CHAPTER 2

1. W. B. Yeats. "Vacillation IV." *The Collected Poems of W. B. Yeats*. New York: Scribner, 1996.

2. Shantideva. *A Guide to the Bodhisattva's Way of Life*. Translated by Stephen Bachelor. Dharmasala, India: Library of Tibetan Works and Archives, 2004.

CHAPTER 5

1. Robert Peter Tristram Coffin. Excerpt from "Crystal Moment."

CHAPTER 6

1. Coleman Barks, trans. Excerpt from "The Mouse and the Camel." *The Essential Rumi*. San Francisco: HarperSanFrancisco, 1995.

2. Dylan Thomas. Excerpt from "Fern Hill." *The Poems of Dylan Thomas*. New York: New Directions, 1971.

CHAPTER 7

1. Kurt Vonnegut. *Slaughterhouse 5, or, the Children's Crusade.* New York: Dell, 1968.

2. William Shakespeare. *Hamlet.*

3. Lord Byron. Canto IV, *Don Juan.*

4. Mitch Albom. *Tuesdays with Morrie.* New York: Doubleday, 1997.

CHAPTER 8

1. Alfred, Lord Tennyson. Excerpt from "In Memoriam," verse 50.

2. William Shakespeare. *Hamlet.* Based on Hamlet's soliloquy: "How all occasions do inform against me."

3. Tom Paxton. "I Can't Help but Wonder Where I'm Bound."

CHAPTER 10

1. Walter Savage Landor. "Dying Speech of an Old Philosopher."

CHAPTER 11

1. See Appendix One.

2. Robert Peter Tristram Coffin. Excerpt from "Crystal Moment."

POSTLUDE

1. Leonard Cohen. "Dance Me to the End of Love."

SELECTED BIBLIOGRAPHY

Books on Alzheimer's

Alterra, Aaron. *The Caregiver: A Life with Alzheimer's.* South Royalton, VT: Steerforth Press, 1999.

Cason, Ann. *Circles of Care: How to Set Up Quality Home Care for Our Elders.* Boston: Shambhala, 2001.

Coste, Joanne Koenig. *Learning to Speak Alzheimer's: A Groundbreaking Approach for Everyone Dealing with the Disease.* New York: Houghton Mifflin, 2003.

DeBaggio, Thomas. *Losing My Mind: An Intimate Look at Life with Alzheimer's.* New York: Free Press, 2002.

Driscoll, Eileen Higgins. *Alzheimer's: A Handbook for the Caretaker.* Boston: Branden Books, 1994.

Gillick, Muriel R. *Tangled Minds: Understanding Alzheimer's Disease and Other Dementias.* New York: Plume, 1999.

Gruetzner, Howard. *Alzheimer's: A Caregiver's Guide and Source Book.* New York: John Wiley & Sons, 1992.

Khalsa, Dharma Singh, with Cameron Stauth. *Brain Longevity*. New York: Warner Books, 1998.

Mace, Nancy L., & Peter V. Rabins. *The 36-Hour Day: A Family Guide to Caring for Persons with Alzheimer's Disease, Related Dementing Illnesses, and Memory Loss in Later Life*. Baltimore: Johns Hopkins Press, 2001.

Miller, Sue. *The Story of My Father*. New York: Knopf, 2003.

Shenk, David. *The Forgetting—Alzheimer's: Portrait of an Epidemic*. New York: Anchor Books, 2001.

Visiting Nurses Association of America. *Caregiver's Handbook: A Complete Guide to Home Health Care*. New York: DK Publishing, 1998.

OTHER HELPFUL BOOKS NOT SPECIFIC TO ALZHEIMER'S

Albom, Mitch. *Tuesdays with Morrie*. New York: Bantam, Doubleday, Dell, 1997.

Chödrön, Pema. *When Things Fall Apart: Heart Advice for Difficult Times*. Boston: Shambhala, 1997.

———*The Places That Scare You: A Guide to Fearlessness in Difficult Times*. Boston: Shambhala, 2001.

Hanh, Thich Nhat. *Being Peace*. Berkeley, Calif.: Parallax Press, 1992.

Kabat-Zinn, Jon. *Wherever You Go There You Are*. New York: Hyperion Books, 1994.

Kornfield, Jack. *A Path with Heart: A Guide through the Perils and Promises of Spiritual Life*. New York: Doubleday, 1993.

Levine, Stephen. *Who Dies? An Investigation of Conscious Living and Dying*. New York: Anchor Books, 1982.

Ram Dass. *Still Here: Embracing Aging, Changing, and Dying*. New York: Riverhead Books, 2000.

Rosenberg, Larry. *Living in the Light of Death: On the Art of Being Truly Alive*. Boston: Shambhala, 2000.

Salzberg, Sharon. *Loving-kindness: The Revolutionary Art of Happiness*. Boston: Shambhala, 1995.

Smith, Rodney. *Lessons from the Dying*. Somerville, Mass.: Wisdom Publications, 1998.

Sogyal Rinpoche. *The Tibetan Book of Living and Dying*. San Francisco: HarperCollins, 1992.

Tulku Thondup. *The Healing Power of Mind*, Boston: Shambhala, 1996.

———— *Peaceful Death, Joyful Rebirth: A Tibetan Buddhist Guidebook*. Boston: Shambhala, 2005.

WEBSITES

The following websites are current as of the publishing date of the book; there may also be new and helpful sites available.

Alzheimer's Association: www.alz.org.
225 North Michigan Avenue, 17th floor, Chicago, IL 60601.
(800) 272-3900.

Alzheimer's Foundation of America: www.alzfdn.org.
322 8th Avenue, 6th floor, New York, NY 10001.
(866) 232-8484.

Alzheimer's Research Foundation: www.alzinfo.org.
One Intrepid Square, New York, NY 10036.
(800) 259-4636.

American Health Assistance Foundation (Alzheimer's Disease Research): www.ahaf.org/alzdis/about/adabout.htm

Mayo Clinic:
www.mayoclinic.com/health/alzheimers/AZ99999

National Institute of Neurological Disorders and Stroke:
www.ninds.nih.gov/disorders/alzheimersdisease/
alzheimersdisease.htm

PBS (The Forgetting, video): www.pbs.org/theforgetting

United States National Institutes of Health:
www.nia.nih.gov/Alzheimers

INDEX

ABOUT THE AUTHOR

Olivia Ames Hoblitzelle is a writer, therapist, and teacher. For over thirty years she has devoted herself to Buddhist practice, which deeply influenced her professional life, in particular how to integrate psychology and meditation.

After practicing as a psychotherapist, she taught in the field of Behavioral Medicine, where she pioneered the integration of meditation, yoga, and cognitive therapy with traditional Western medicine. While teaching at the Mind/Body Medical Institute, she also developed training programs for health professionals in new approaches to health and healing through Harvard Medical School. During her career she has educated people in contemplative practices in a wide variety of settings: government agencies, businesses, hospitals, organizations, churches, and most extensively in school systems.

As part of her commitment to contemplative life, Olivia has served on the boards of three organizations whose missions are to encourage and deepen Buddhist practices in the West: Insight Meditation Society, Trijang Buddhist Institute, and Dharma Friends. With her enduring commitment to peace and social justice, she was a founding board member of the Karuna Center for Peacebuilding.

Now an elder with two grown children and four grandsons, she lives in Massachusetts and spends as much time as she can in Vermont where she grows vegetables, welcomes family and friends, and steeps herself in the glories of nature. Olivia continues to teach, counsel, and write.

Olivia Hoblitzelle offers talks and workshops on the following topics:

* Aging: The Gifts of Adversity

* The Majesty of Your Loving: Reflections on Mental Diminishment

* Meditation and the Healing Mind

* Heart Instructions on Living and Dying

* Telling Our Stories: Spirituality and Life Review

Info@MajestyofYourLoving.com
P.O. Box 381487
Cambridge, MA 02238-1487

Please visit
www.MajestyofYourLoving.com
for more information.